SUSTAINABLE
SAILING

SUSTAINABLE SAILING

Go Green When You Cast Off

DIETER LOIBNER

SHERIDAN HOUSE

Published 2009 by
Sheridan House Inc.
145 Palisade Street
Dobbs Ferry, NY 10522
www.sheridanhouse.com

Library of Congress Cataloging-in-Publication Data

Loibner, Dieter
    Sustainable sailing : go green when you cast off / Dieter Loibner.
        p. cm.
    Includes index.
    ISBN 978-1-57409-284-4 (pbk. : alk. paper)
    1. Sailing. 2. Sailing—Environmental aspects. 3. Sustainable
living. 4. Green movement. I. Title.
    GV811.L65 2009
    797.124—dc22   2009038366

ISBN 978 1 57409 284 4

Printed in the United States of America

You can't protect what you don't understand.
Dan Haifley,
executive director O'Neill Sea Odyssey

Contents

Foreword

I met Dieter Loibner in 2005 while testing crew overboard equipment on San Francisco Bay. He was very engaged in this particular challenge and reported extensively on the findings. So when he asked me to write the foreword for *Sustainable Sailing* I was very excited, because I knew Dieter would approach the complex topic of sustainability with the same intense curiosity.

Whether we sail, fish, kayak or powerboat the water is a part of us. As boaters, we have a close relationship with the rivers, bays and oceans that ebb and flow through our lives. With a quote from President John F. Kennedy, Dieter reminds us that we have the same percentage of salt in our bodies as in the ocean. How could we not want our waterways to thrive? He pushes us to understand our impact on the environment. We may not agree with everything he says or be able to embrace every suggestion tomorrow, but if we are to continue to enjoy our water world we need to start changing how we do things.

As I read this book, I felt overwhelmed at times by the challenges we face. As president of the BoatU.S. Foundation for Boating Safety and Clean Water I know how hard it can be to change behavior. It is what we strive for every day. We have been educating boaters about environmentally sound practices for over 15 years. Through our outreach on topics such as clean fueling, invasive species prevention, and marine debris, we constantly touch boaters around the country daily. We have awarded hundreds of thousands of dollars in grant funding to local communities and provided marinas and local boating groups with the resources they need to educate boaters on minimizing their environmental impacts.

But we are not alone in our efforts, Dieter explains how engineers, scientists, lawyers, designers, and builders are working on ways to make boating greener. New materials and products are being tested and improved everyday. Dieter introduces us to the movers and shakers in the boating community and the industry. He shares with us their solutions and challenges. Innovations in fuels, boats, batteries, solar panels, wind and water generators are helping already. Some of these products are within our reach and others are still a ways off. Cost is a factor for most boaters, especially during these challenging times, so finding cost-effective solutions is imperative to the adoption of many of these technologies.

While this book focuses on sustainable sailing, sailors comprise only 20 percent of the boating population. To truly make an impact, we need to cast a larger net and challenge all boaters, power and sail, towards sustainability. I enjoy sailing and power boating and believe cleaner power boating is attainable. Diesel-electric, hybrid propulsion and solar energy are catching on. Smaller, long-range trawlers that consume less fuel are becoming more popular. Alternative fuels will likely become more prevalent over the next 10 years. Obviously, there are no silver bullets but the times are a-changing.

I am a great believer in grassroots efforts. Ultimately, the future of our planet comes down to people. Individuals taking responsibility and action to clean up our waterways can make an incredible difference. Many of us have become comfortable greening our homes, so it is only natural to extend this drive to our activities on the water. As we become more comfortable doing things "the green way," I believe the future will be cleaner and brighter, but this process has to start with awareness.

Sustainable Sailing is a comprehensive book on the environmental effects of not just sailing and the boating industry but the impact of our boating culture on our world. It offers readers insight on boat design, construction and operation. Dieter makes suggestions on how to turn sailing into a more sustainable activity, from modifying personal behavior to commissioning a carbon neutral custom yacht and everything in between. By putting it all in one place he's done us a great favor.

Ruth Wood
President, BoatU.S. Foundation
for Boating Safety and Clean Water

SUSTAINABLE SAILING

Introduction

It was at the Better Living show in Portland, Oregon that it finally sunk in: Green will be the new normal. Recession aside, the sustainability revolution was on display in full splendor and it looked like it was gathering speed: Wind generators, eco-houses, electric cars, earth-friendly backrubs and potions, organic pretzels and beer brewed with solar power. It was an amazing array of products and services. You can even die green and go to heaven in an eco-coffin. Why, then, I asked myself, shouldn't there be a movement that promotes sustainable sailing? Why not, indeed?

Before we get to the details, I would like to establish the case for a book like this. I am not a firebrand naturalist or environmentalist, but I do believe in the importance of resources management, reducing environmental impact and giving Homo sapiens a chance to live up to his name. Like other parents, I'd like for my daughter to inherit a livable planet with sufficient and healthy resources, which won't happen if we let things slide the way we have.

Nature doesn't need to be saved for its own sake. If we succeed in destroying our environment, it'll still be nature, but most likely minus man. Earth will still be a planet, but one that is inhospitable to our existence. "Nature does not teach its creatures to control their appetites except by the harshest of lessons—epidemics, mass death, extinctions," Michael Pollan wrote in *Second Nature*. "Nothing would be more natural than for humankind to burden the environment to the extent that it was rendered unfit for human life."

After decades of downplaying or ignoring critical science, political protraction and industrial opposition, society is waking up to the consequences of unsustainable practices. Awareness is the first step, but it won't stop the environmental clock from ticking louder and faster, with more people consuming more and throwing away more. It's our watch and we need to adjust the course, which means shifting our thinking from short-term gain to long-term sustainability and changing behavior from short-sighted linear consumption to a resource-conscious pattern of reducing, reusing and recycling. We have to remind ourselves that nobody gets a free lunch. The bills for our depredations will come due, whether we pay them or our descendants. It is true that the power of the sun is free and it makes things grow through photosynthesis, turning the vegetable garden in my backyard into a jungle of berries, tomatoes, squash and zucchini, thus adding to the biomass instead of depleting it.

As sailors we know the power of the sun's renewable energy because we depend on it, not because we have to, but we want to. It generates wind and wind generates the power for sails, so yes, sailing actually is a step ahead of the game.

Sailing a small boat across a big ocean also can be a metaphor for a sustainable lifestyle, because it is a microcosm that mimics Mother Earth. It's an instructive experience in thinking ahead and adjusting consumption to available supplies, so that everybody on board might have enough—and that's the operative word—to make the trip in comfort, not in gluttony. If 30 gallons of water have to last a crew of two for a 15 day-passage, it's a gallon per person per day, period. If the crew needs more, it has to be bunkered or manufactured from seawater, which has its own implications for equipment and energy supply. It all has to be considered before the trip even starts.

However, when it comes to environmental stewardship, we sailors are no saints. We pump sewage overboard and operate diesel and gasoline engines that pollute water and air. We use toxic paints to retard marine growth and aggressive cleaning products. We succumb to "gadgetritis," which causes the demand for electric energy on board to skyrocket, and we surround ourselves with items that have been designed and built for a linear system with no place to go but into the landfill once they are at the end of their useful life.

We as sailors have interest in and knowledge of the aquatic environment, which is the source of our mental and physical recreation.

Therefore we have a moral obligation to help protect and restore what we proclaim to love. If this book can inspire the adoption of better practices in only one facet, be it trash reduction, water conservation, or head etiquette, and encourage others to try it too, it will make a modest contribution to the upside by promoting awareness and solutions. If some of that might seem a bit hackneyed, that's a wager I take, because that's also part of the new normal: thinking outside the box, reaching out to the unusual, getting comfortable with stuff that looks and works differently. Never underestimate the power of change, even in sailing, which prides itself on tradition. As recently as 1995, who'd have thought of a rookie team from a small landlocked country like Switzerland winning the America's Cup? Yet it happened, simply because rules and conditions changed.

Pollution is personal

I was raised on the old continent, one stop farther east from Switzerland, in Austria, where environmental issues were mostly settled through the heavy hand of government. But when disaster hit, it hit close to home, so citizens paid attention and favored measures that promised a modicum of protection against the consequences. Perhaps one of the most severe such incidents occurred in December of 1952, when a toxic mix of dense fog and sooty coal smoke killed thousands of people in London. It's known as the Killer Fog of '52 and still ranks up there with the deadliest environmental calamities. One of the first stories about an environment under siege that I personally remember was the toxic smoke that blanketed North Rhine Westphalia, an industrial area of Germany where people mined coal and milled steel. Through war and peace, heavy industries dominated the area. Profit ruled, concern for nature (or workers) was a pesky distraction. But those smokestacks emitted sulfur dioxide in high concentrations, which made people sick. Tough luck, if you lived in this area. But once it became clear that this stuff travels in the form of acid rain that damaged rivers, lakes and forests hundreds of miles away, the problem took on a larger footprint.

Then there's 1976, the year that my childhood idol, Franz Klammer, won the skiing downhill Gold medal at the winter Olympics in spectacular fashion. The following summer I started sailing a Laser, which was a hoot, but that was overshadowed by a scare that came from Northern Italy: A few miles outside Milan, one of the most populous cities there, a chemical plant exploded. The catastrophe of Seveso, as the incident became known, sent a cloud of dioxin, widely believed to be one of the most toxic man-made chemicals, into the atmosphere. Ten years later, during my college days in Vienna, several hundred miles to the east, in today's Ukraine the nuclear reactor of Chernobyl melted down. The fire sent a plume of radioactive fallout into the atmosphere that was 400 times more concentrated than the fallout from the Hiroshima bombing. The Soviet regime tried to censor the coverage of the disaster, but when the plume drifted west it made radioactive rain fall as far away as Ireland. More than 300,000 people had to be evacuated and resettled. "If you start glowing in the dark," one crude joke suggested, "it's time to check into the hospital."

Less lethal, but still annoying were the frequent and widespread algal blooms of the 1970s and 80s. They were caused by industrial and agricultural runoff and forced the closure of hundreds of beaches in the northern Adriatic. For us kids it was a tragedy, because the seaside vacation was canceled. No swimming, no sailing, no fun.

During the 1982 European Championship regatta in the Finn Dinghy class in El Masnou, Spain, I had an exclusive encounter with pollution. The race course was a couple of miles offshore, in plain sight of the industrial port of Barcelona, 10 miles to the south. I had a brand new sail and faint hopes to finish somewhere in the middle of the fleet. Things weren't looking too bad in the first race when I found myself reaching toward the gybe mark. Suddenly, the water became oddly calm without any drop in wind speed and it started to smell like someone was paving a road. I was sailing through an oil slick. Not being very experienced in the Finn or in sailing on open ocean water, I had my hands full. To make matters worse, reading the water for puffs on an oil slick is impossible, because there's no ripple on the surface. One such puff got the better of me. It was a classic crash to windward: Full-tilt, back first into the drink. The boat turned turtle instantaneously and the race was over. By the time I had the thin end pointing upward again, I was nauseous and looked like a grease monkey. The formerly snow-white Line 7 overalls were full of smelly brown grime and my new sail a disgrace. "Oh that always happens when they flush the tanks in Barcelona Harbor and we get a sea breeze," one of the locals told me later.

Getting marinated in crude while sailing is a transforming experience. The victim's perspective was unique. I had my fill of oil spills for life. But in the sense of full disclosure I need to share an episode that features yours truly as perpetrator. It occurred on my dad's cruising catamaran, off the coast of Croatia ca. 1974. The honey bucket, a small lime green port-a-potty had reached capacity and needed to be emptied. It was a warm and windless day in August and I drew the short straw to handle the task of dumping the contents of the holding tank over the stern. That's how you did it then, simply because there were no marinas or pump-out facilities available. While the rest of the crew smirked and joked about latrine management, I toiled. It was a small crapper, but the holding tank was filled to the brim, so it was heavy. Gritting my teeth, I yanked it off the pedestal down below, lugged it up the companionway, to the back of the deck that was not secured by lifelines. There I unscrewed the discharge cap, tilted the apparatus and started pouring. Omygod! It was at the bottom of the fun scale, around root canal without Novocain. "Let it be over, please," was all I could think, while I tilted it some more to speed up the process. Well, haste makes waste. The thing slipped and before I knew what was happening, the potty took me for a dive. I spare you the gory details, except that I stayed under water for a long time. When I had to come up for air, you can guess my first thought. The second was: "Keep your head up and your mouth shut." And for once in my life I really did. Sure, I had this coming to me. I was a gutless guppy for dumping the holding tank in a reckless fashion. In my defense I can argue that my hand was forced by the lack of tidy solutions to the problem at the time. But nearly four decades later, things haven't really changed all that much in many popular charter venues around the world. There are marinas and thousands of charter boats that fan out over the islands in the Adriatic, in the Caribbean or in the South Pacific, but people still dump their holding tanks (if they even have them) close to shore, by ignorance or lack of alternatives.

So my experiences helped sharpen my sensitivity toward the environment, on and off the water. But making sustainability a principle that guides thinking and behavior is not as simple as installing a software upgrade on your computer. It has been a continuing process and there are no patented solutions that work equally well for everyone, because there are endless permutations of sustainable behavior. "It is what you want it to be," a friend once told me. "But it is incumbent on every person to take the initiative and figure out what works best."

How green is sailing?

Everybody knows that the best cure for seasickness is sitting under a tree. But as a part-time gardener (actually the source of cheap labor) I found similarities between garden work and boating. Pushing the mechanical mower to cut unruly grass, I often wondered why. Lawns require irrigation, fertilizer and regular care. It's pure slavery and often an egregious waste of water. If people don't do it themselves, they have to hire what my wife and I call the "hoe-mow-blow-and-go brigade." A green lawn makes a mockery of Green as a sustainable principle, at least in arid and semi-arid climates. Gardening on the other hand, if it respects climate and geography, can be an example for sustainability: Planting native plants instead of coddling thirsty lawns, spreading compost instead of chemical fertilizer that poisons the run-off, drip irrigation instead of spraying fountains, and eschewing the armada of motorized tools.

I think about sailing as tending to a garden and power boating as tending to a lawn. One is only possible if the operator has help from technology and petrochemicals. The other takes advantage of clean, renewable energy that is available on the spot and for free, and rewards those who are willing to adjust to the rhythms and moods of nature. Like gardening, sailing requires skill, patience, and effort while building a keen sense of place, as anybody can confirm who has sailed in different venues and dealt with different wind and weather patterns.

Trying to define sustainability in a social and economic context and as a desirable attribute for sailing, I thought of conscious consumption, and the resulting consequences. It implies using resources responsibly with minimum impact on the environment and others. But sustainability also means getting collateral benefits from sensible practices. Something for nothing, like a workout and a free parking spot if I spare the air and take the bike. That's heady stuff and might cause some chuckles, but some day sustainable will be the norm and unsustainable the exception. As it stands now, it's still a choice not a mandate. Persistent education will help, as long as it highlights sustainable solutions that are true alternatives for everyone and supports informed decision-making on the part of the consumer. So here, without particular ranking, are some of the issues that deserve consideration for sustainable thinking and living on the water or on dry land:

There's the rush and the time pressure that follows us from land to sea, turning sailboats into powerboats with a mast and a keel, just so one can get there "on time." But what if the boat was performing better in a wider range of conditions, would it cut back the use of the engine? If we are less ambitious in our itineraries and more inclined to use Zen as our operating manual, if we didn't cover X amount of miles in Y amount of time, wouldn't we be sailing more? "Out of principle, TABOO III does not operate under engine," veteran circumnavigator and catamaran cruiser Wolfgang Hausner wrote in response to the question when sailing becomes motoring. " The boat moves in the slightest of breezes and to me even one knot of speed through the water is sailing."

Electric and electronic gadgets have a voracious appetite for power that needs to be satisfied somehow. Mostly that means plugging into a convenient shore power connection, but where does the power come from? Chances are it is generated a few hundred miles away, possibly by a coal-fired power plant that spews thousands of tons of greenhouse gasses into the atmosphere to feed the grid with electricity. There is more bad news: While it is en route from the point of generation to your boat, a great portion of electrical power is lost through transmission inefficiencies.

Heads are coming to a head. Even if it is not a port-a-john that goes by the board with a clumsy deckhand, a ship's toilet is still messy, and when it breaks it is one of the least popular items on any skipper's fix-it list. Yet we all have to use it and flush it. But flushing doesn't end the story. Once sewage leaves the boat it can easily turn into a mess on a grand scale. It is an emotional and deeply personal issue. Depending on where you sail, there can be tight regulations for the treatment and disposal of sewage, or it's a free-for-all. Either way, finding the golden compromise that reprieves the environment without spoiling the experience is possible with a collaborative approach.

Inevitably, sailors also have to deal with non-biodegradable waste such as engine oil or plastic packaging. Plastic is practical and convenient, but simply tossing it into the garbage or even recycling it won't make it go away, as anyone can testify who's ever seen the endless parade of bottles, caps, lighters, shopping bags and other detritus heading out to sea on an ebb tide. There it accumulates and kills marine life, but also breaks down into small and toxic pieces that get into the food chain, which means that the problem we created and tried to put out of sight and out of mind is headed back to haunt us at the dinner table. Plastic, of course, also is the building material of choice for most pleasure boats. It is easy to use in mass production, it is durable and easy to maintain, but it is also quite difficult to turn into something else once a boat is being scrapped. Humans may have "environmentally sustainable end-of-life options" (see www.ecoffinsusa.com), but for a sailboat that's a much more difficult proposition.

Antifouling paints that keep the bottom of a boat tidy are getting some attention these days. After tin-based paints were banned in most places, copper is coming under scrutiny, because studies have shown that it accumulates at high concentrations in the ground sediment of poorly flushed marina basins, which can have deleterious effects on marine life.

Gas-guzzlers are out, not just since a wave of bankruptcies has swept through the U.S. auto industry. For the last decade and a half, the EPA has steadily tightened fuel efficiency and emissions standards for combustion engines and what applies to cars will apply to boats, eventually. Catalytic converters, particle filters, and common-rail injection are rapidly becoming standard for marine engines. It makes them cleaner, but also more expensive. All good reasons for setting sail and sheeting in.

Cost is a valid concern too, especially in times of recession when cash is tight and businesses are looking to cut back rather than investing. Implementing cradle-to-cradle sustainability (i.e. making new boats from old ones) requires money, innovation and coordination between government, industry and consumers. It permeates all aspects of a product's life cycle, from design and procurement of materials to manufacturing and end-of-use options, including recycling and disposal strategies. If sustainability pundits are right, ecological and social responsibility will be critical for economic success, because customers demand products that match their personal and environmental ethics.

Apropos ecological and social responsibility: "Made in China" with all its advantages and challenges will take on a different quality, literally and figuratively. Cheap and abundant labor and lower production cost have attracted thousands of companies, who now get some or all of their goods, including boats and boating gear, produced there. It's not what China makes, but how it makes it, using electricity that comes from highly polluting coal-fired power plants. That's one of the reasons why Made in China still is cheap. However, as the country's wealth increases, its environment continues to suffer and the effects are felt around the world, because pollution travels. As China's largest customer, the U.S. asked the government to step up its efforts to reduce greenhouse gases, but it's a slippery political issue. First, because better technology is more expensive, which erodes the bottom line of cheap mass-produced goods. Second, because industrialized nations who built their wealth on pollution, lack moral authority. Yet China (and India, too) have to be on board if confronting climate change is to stand a chance.

People, planet, profit

While the link between ecology and economy has yet to change the way most boating business operate (an industry white paper that was published in November of 2008 mentioned the term "eco-friendly" only once and in passing), other outdoor industries already have taken this step, because customers demand ecological and social responsibility. Keeping investors and the public informed about progress in this respect, requires a commitment to transparency in reporting and the understanding of the triple bottom line: People, planet, profit.

A company that has recognized the environmental bent in their customers as early as the 1970s and took the initiative with defining and establishing positive business practices for the outdoor industry is Patagonia, an apparel and sportswear manufacturer with headquarters in Ventura, California. "Our definition of quality includes a mandate for building products and working with processes that cause the least harm to the environment. We evaluate raw materials, invest in innovative technologies, rigorously police our waste and use a portion of our sales to support groups working to make a real difference," Patagonia says. What started as a grassroots effort now is a juggernaut of initiatives that also inspired some nautical companies such as retail giant West Marine, and the Olympic Circle Sailing Club in Berkeley, California, who promote economic and social responsibility as part of their mission statement.

Patagonia pledges at least 1 percent of sales or 10 percent of pretax profits to environmental groups. So far, the company says, it has given more than $31 million in grants and in-kind donations to more than 1,000 organizations. Patagonia also founded the Conservation Alliance, which grew to 155 member companies who are involved in environmental work for the benefit of nature and their business. Each member contributes annual dues to a central fund, which then is being donated to grassroots environmental groups. According to a published report, the Conservation Alliance donated $800,000 to 29 organizations in 2007 and the tally of grants over the previous 20 years has surpassed $6.5 million. However, giving green and going green are two different pairs of shoes, so Patagonia tried to set an example with their own corporate conduct by committing to garment recycling, the use of solar power and Leadership in Energy and Environmental Design (LEED) certification from the U.S. Green Building Council (USGBC) for office and warehouse buildings. The charter company Sunsail received a gold-level LEED certification from the U.S. Building council for their Clearwater, Florida headquarters.

Talking green is cool, but talk alone won't bring change. At one point we have to take the initiative and the best way to start is with the individual that stares back at us from the mirror. "I live, therefore I pollute," said Cap'n Fatty Goodlander, paraphrasing Descartes without a hint of shame in his voice. He's in his fifth decade of living aboard and circling the planet on his own keel and knows a thing or two about sustainable living on a boat, since that's the only way to do it for as long as he's done it and with as little as he's spent. Goodlander has cultivated a large following among sailing folks with his humorous and often self-deprecating accounts of things that can and will go wrong in the life of a salt-stained sea gypsy. "Where there used to be three boats in an anchorage, there are 300 now," he says. "Numbers impact the environment as much as [bad] practices. But there is also peer pressure. Someone who threw a can overboard might have found imitators in the past. It bred bad habits. Now it's time to turn it around and let peer pressure breed positive habits. If you toss a beer can over the side in a regatta that's sponsored by a beer company, and you get caught, you get disqualified." But Goodlander is not one of the eco-Nazis. He understands that goodwill and a friendly approach work much better than coercive strategies. Nobody is a saint, so it's important to cut others some slack, especially in remote areas where indigenous people strive to attain the Western lifestyle. "Don't be a hypocrite and lecture them about sustainability from the deck of your yacht when they pollute less in their lifetime than you did just by visiting them," Goodlander explains.

A casual, friendly and non-controversial approach is what non-profit organizations such as Save Our Shores teach their volunteers when they approach boaters in their outreach efforts. "Please introduce your information in a manner that acknowledges boaters as the experts they are. Try to present information in a way that appeals to their interests," suggests the training manual for the DockWalker program that educates boaters about the use of oil absorbent pads and bilge pumps to prevent oil pollution. Nudging people toward behavioral change and conscious consumption might be the cheapest and most effective way to reduce environmental impact, but it is also a delicate matter. There are several reasons for this, some rooted in human nature that resists change, or in resentment. The other challenge is the ambivalence of many boating executives, who privately agree that the age of excess probably is over and that the industry is undergoing profound changes. But wearing their business hats, they are still somewhat hesitant to join the party, because few have yet figured out how to sell less of what they make and still turn a profit.

Regardless of the economic cycle, society will have to learn to manage environment and natural resources in the face of dwindling supplies and rising demand. Combined with tougher environmental legislation this will stoke the demand for sustainable practices and eco-friendly products, and boating isn't exempt. It might not be at the top of anyone's agenda in Washington, but the marine industry has to reinvent itself to remain relevant with products that satisfy the customer (people), the environmental aspect (planet), and the bottom line (profit). It's a process that's been underway for a while.

"They said it couldn't be done. More than a decade ago, when the EPA told outboard builders it was time to clean up their emissions act, manufacturers predicted it would be the ruination of the sport, that consumers would never buy a heavy, expensive, and unreliable low-emissions outboard," *Boating's* Charles Pluddemann wrote in a 2007 story about catalytic converters. "They complained loud and hard, but eventually the transition was made to the clean, quiet, and more-efficient two- and four-stroke outboards we enjoy today." The same pattern developed when the California Air Resources Board mandated a 75-percent reduction in hydrocarbon and nitrogen oxide emissions, which required gasoline inboard engines to be fitted with catalytic converters. "Again, the hue and cry was deafening: 'You can't put a blazing-hot catalytic converter in an engine room.' Most engine marinizers said it couldn't, or shouldn't, be done," Pluddemann wrote. But in 2007, Indmar Marine introduced the first marine inboard fitted with an exhaust catalyst system. A year later, Volvo Penta and MerCruiser followed suit.

Even though the sustainability movement in the boating industry still has to reach the tipping point, efforts are becoming more noticeable. A few ripples here, a few ripples there, and before long there will be a steady breeze that signifies that Green indeed is the new normal.

Sizing Up the Issues

At the America Cup dinner given by the Australian ambassador in Newport, Rhode Island, on September 14, 1962, the night before the first race of the eighteenth America's Cup, President John F. Kennedy addressed the guests: "I really don't know why it is that all of us are so committed to the sea, except I think it is because in addition to the fact that the sea changes and the light changes, and ships change, it is because we all came from the sea. And it is an interesting biological fact that all of us have, in our veins the exact same percentage of salt in our blood that exists in the ocean, and, therefore, we have salt in our blood, in our sweat, in our tears. We are tied to the ocean. And when we go back to the sea, whether it is to sail or to watch it we are going back from whence we came."

Kennedy, himself a keen sailor, was acutely aware of the relationship between man and sea, whether on a sailboat or not. Oceans cover 70 percent of the planet. That's a lot of water and one huge playground for sailors. But oceans also are gigantic ecosystems that have many vital functions. They brew the weather, they absorb greenhouse gases from the atmosphere, they provide food, they create jobs and they are a favorite place for millions who seek renewal and recreation. Oceans are vital to all of us. Therefore logic suggests that it would be a good idea to keep such an important resource healthy and balanced. But Homo sapiens isn't doing such a good job: He's exploiting fisheries faster than they can recover; he's dumping sewage, oil, plastic, toxins and garbage in unprecedented amounts;

he's changing the climate which alters sea levels, water temperature and acidity. And all of that has far-reaching implications, because it all works synergistically. Once the system is completely out of whack, there's no telling how it can be re-aligned.

If oceans had the litigious disposition of humans, they would be in a court of law to seek restitution and punitive damages. But they don't need lawyers to argue their case. They react to man's meddling without malice, without revenge. Once all sea life is gone or inedible and the oceans' surface temperature has risen enough so that the planet's climate will be completely turned on its head, man will be the one who suffers most. We have the intellectual capacity to recognize the nature of the problems, how they develop and what the likely consequences are. We also have the scientific tools to tally the damage that's been done so far, from the ocean's floor to the stratosphere. But we appear oddly hamstrung when it comes to taking decisive action. Environmental damage and loss of biodiversity are becoming increasingly intolerable as the price for economic growth. Healthy ecosystems, strong economies and thriving communities depend on and sustain each other. It's not just a new way or a better way, but it's the only way if we want to conserve the environment for future generations.

As much as we like to think about technology as a savior, the inconvenient truth is that habits will have to be adjusted, too. And how rapidly habits shift, given the right circumstances, became evident in 2007 when fuel prices inexorably climbed toward $4 per gallon. The Department of Transportation reported that Americans had driven 30 billion fewer miles on public roads over the previous 6 months and sales of midsize SUVs were down 38 percent. When credit became tight, even big spenders started pinching pennies, boosting the personal savings rate from 0.1 percent in March of 2008 to five percent a year later, according to a report by Marketwatch. As a consequence, luxury items such as boats practically went out of style. In 2009, some manufacturers reported sales decreases of 40 to 50 percent or more.

However there is good news for the environment: People who buy less throw away less. Oregon's Department of Environmental Quality, for instance, reported a 16-percent decline in landfill waste at the end of 2008. Economy can be a big motivator for behavioral change, but it's also coercive, so it wasn't likely going to last. As soon as gas prices dropped, sales figures for large vehicles started to climb again.

The value of green

"There is nothing more powerful than inspirational leadership that unleashes principled behavior for a great cause," Dov Seidman told New York Times columnist Thomas Friedman. Seidman is the C.E.O. of LRN, a company that helps inspire principled performance in business, and the author of the book "How." Adding more coercive rules and regulations to control behaviors, Seidman explained, doesn't make a company or a government more sustainable. "Laws tell you what you can do. Values inspire in you what you should do."

Take the Toyota Prius. It's arguably the most successful hybrid car, not just because of its technology that combines electric and gasoline propulsion, but also for its distinctively different look that proclaim efficiency in almost every detail. However even high fuel prices don't justify the purchase of such a vehicle because hybrid technology is still expensive. But that's missing the point: "A Prius is not about saving money," Paul Mika once told me. He is the owner of the Toyota dealership in Middletown, Rhode Island, and he should know. "It is about making a statement." Driving a Prius advertises that doing the right thing is more important to the owner than simple math. How difficult then, could it be to elevate sailboats to this kind of lofty symbolism, given that they are much greener than a hybrid car that still has to burn gas to function.

Industry captains at the Responsible Business Summit 2009 in London weighed in on corporate responsibility and "Climate Change Strategy: why producing cost-effective green products is your best bet yet." Discussion focused on how to make cost-effective green products, how to keep the supply chain green, and how to develop viable sustainability strategies, because in the long run, climate change legislation, volatile energy prices, and high customer interest in green products will make (or keep) sustainability a top priority of the corporate agenda.

The debate of sustainability strategies is not limited to Fortune 500 companies. In the U.S., the Outdoor Industry Association founded the Eco Working Group in 2007 with more than 80 businesses that collaborate to develop an "Eco Index," an assessment tool that provides environmental guidelines, performance metrics and a comparative benchmark scoring system to measure a manufacturer's environmental footprint. Members include companies such as 3M, Adidas, Keen, K2, Nike, Patagonia, REI, Timberland and several non-profits. Among them is one outfit that's deeply rooted in leisure boating: Helly Hansen, a supplier of foul weather gear.

Consumers are becoming increasingly eco-savvy, demanding more sustainable practices from the companies, so the Outdoors Industry Association and its members were able to stay ahead of the curve. Standardizing tools to measure the global impact of manufacturing and business practices, combating "green fatigue," which is a symptom of invalidated environmental claims, lack of transparency and insufficient education, and preempting mandatory government standards for eco-indexing are at the top of the agenda. EWG members also pool resources for better pricing when procuring sustainable materials, which in turn helps make their products more affordable.

While collaborating, EWG members are also fierce competitors, who seize marketing opportunities when they see them, i.e. by "outbehaving" others. Keen, the maker of the Newport sandal, popular with boaters, issued a report card on social and environmental progress and disclosed that in 2007, the delivery of more than 3 million pairs of shoes to U.S. retail outlets caused more than 6,000 metric tons of carbon dioxide emissions. "We are a young company that was founded in this millennium, so sustainability is in our DNA," said Chris Enlow, the sustainability officer of Keen. "From the U.S. president on down, the new code of conduct includes transparency and accountability and we want customers who support companies that conduct themselves responsibly." Participating in the Eco Working Group, Enlow explains, makes sense on different levels, because it fosters engagement and collaboration. "It's engage or lose. We are sitting around the same table and learn to speak a common language. Not just among each other, but also to the outside, and especially suppliers." The goal is the development of a scoring system that allows vendors to grade their products on an eco-friendliness scale. To get there, it is important to understand the lifecycle of each product and the carbon footprint it produces.

The boating industry is still trying to rally its constituents for far-reaching sustainability initiatives, grappling with fragmentation, an economic down-cycle, resistance to change and the challenge of putting a green label on powerboats, which make up the vast majority of vessels sold in the US. *Sailors for the Sea*, a non-profit that was founded by philanthropist David Rockefeller Jr., and advocates a combination of sailing and marine conservation, initiated the Certified Sea Friendly program in 2009. The goal was to start an industry dialogue to develop boats that are more eco-friendly in design, construction, use, and disposal. It's still a long way to product stewardship or extended producer responsibility, such as it is practiced by electronic companies that take back products at the end of their useful lives.

But perhaps one day boats will be recycled. Unless the industry returns to wooden hulls and cotton sails (perhaps an intriguing thought for some), it will take a lot of collaboration and innovation, because processes will have to be changed and managed differently, materials will have to be engineered to provide higher value than ground-up fiberglass recyclate currently does. And there will have to be a way to pay for it. Yes, fiberglass boats last much longer than cars or sneakers, as John McKnight, the director of environmental and safety compliance at the National Marine Manufacturers Association pointed out, but implementing sustainable boat recycling or disposal programs seems as much a technical as a political issue. "I personally dislike government intervention, [but] the truth is that the only real changes have been triggered by political mandate," stated Wolfgang Unger, the president of Seawolf Design, Inc., a company that specializes in composite fabrication and fiberglass recycling equipment.

On the retail end, West Marine has been leading the charge, driven by founder and chairman Randy Repass, who now splits his time between bluewater cruising and supporting conservation efforts. "There are several things happening that will shape the future of boating in a positive way," he said. "There are green products on display at boat shows. *Sailors for the Sea* is educating folks about recycling and conservation issues, and plans to develop guidelines and certification for green boats." Repass always was ahead of the curve. He has lived off the grid in the Santa Cruz Mountains for decades. Back in the early 1980s when green was not even a faint glimmer and West Marine opened its Santa Cruz, California warehouse, he insisted on installing skylights in the roof to admit more natural light to reduce the need for electric lighting. In 2003, West Marine installed a 57-kilowatt photovoltaic system on the roof of the company's Santa Cruz retail store with 480 120-watt solar panels that produce more than 300 kWh of electricity per day, equal to 54 percent of the 7,500-square-foot store's needs. On a dedicated solar Web site, www.westmarinesolar.com, the company said that the accrued savings of the first 20 days of operation amounted to $800, and the equivalent of 10 barrels of oil or 1.5 tons of CO_2.

As positive as the use of solar energy to power a retail store is, it can't hide the fact that many boating products the company sells are not exactly green, i.e. paints, solvents, motor oil and fuel additives. Several years ago, West Marine undertook an effort to market maintenance products that were labeled as biodegradable, but abandoned the practice, for the lack of credible standards. Now eco-friendly is back. "We have adopted the Design for the Environment (a program by the Environmental Protection Agency) to certify sustainable products," Repass pointed out (see Chapter 10). "And we also issue an environmental report card to show how we are reducing the carbon footprint with a more fuel-efficient fleet of delivery trucks and saving on utilities."

Others were less enthusiastic about answering questions regarding their sustainability efforts or providing data that quantifies the positive impact through recycling, waste reduction or emissions control in their factories. Only one builder's CEO, Michael Schmidt from Hanse Yachts in Germany, fashioned a response that summarized his company's activities for more sustainable production methods such as water-based paints and closed-loop recycling during production. However, he also acknowledged there's a need to do more, especially regarding the disposal of old boats.

The bottom line: Many boating industry executives know that sustainability is the future, but few have made the leap. "Engage or lose" is more than deft sloganeering. It is the recognition that sitting back means being left behind. But it all starts with a big table and a lot of chairs, Repass suggested. "Cooperation can happen, all the involved groups need to sit down and get to know each other."

Sailors for sustainability

Sailors, who have a pinch more salt in their bodies than regular folks (at least figuratively), have a special relationship to the sea. It is their playground after all, and to move their boats, they depend on the source of renewable energy that sustains life. In its purest form, sailing uses "fuel from heaven," where sun (and wind) come from, rather than "fuel from hell," where oil, gas and coal originate. Sailing also is a rewarding activity, because it requires a variety of skills to get from Point A to Point B. To say nothing about intangibles like the satisfaction of making good time under canvas; the relaxation that comes with silence, the invigorating fresh air and the reward of being a part of undisturbed nature. Sailors are ideal advocates for sustainable behavior that can inspire others.

Conservation efforts by sailors are not a novel idea, but lately they gain more visibility if not funding. They are propelled by unnamed volunteers, the unsung heroes who donate thousands of hours of their time and a great deal of sweat, but also by high-profile leaders like Rockefeller who has been a sailor for most of his life, mucking around on dinghies in his youth, graduating to keel boats and eventually landing a spot on 12-Meter yachts that were vying for a spot in the America's Cup. Later he served on the Pew Oceans Commission, which studied pollution, coastal development, and overfishing. He co-wrote the commission's report, a landmark document that put the spotlight on the issues scientists and environmentalists have been warning about for years. Next, Rockefeller connected the dots by linking his sailing passion to the sustainability agenda. In 2004, he founded *Sailors for the Sea*, "to build the constituency of boaters and sailors that I felt would be necessary to help educate the public, and activate and motivate the boating community," as he said in a blog on the Cruising World Web site.

The hope is to tap into the potential of approximately 3.5 million sailors in this country (according to an aggregated demographic compiled by industry organizations for the year 2006), and turning them into ambassadors for the cause. Perhaps it would be more prudent to go with the hard core, the one million sailors who said they went out 15 times or more that year. They have stronger ties to the sport than casual practitioners and more of a vested interest in environmental health, since they will be out there again and again. Even if only five percent of all boating participants (ca. 60 million in 2007) are sailing, it's a minority that has clout. Here are some reasons why sailors are well suited to become advocates and activists for the cause:

- Sailors are passionate. They are involved in clubs or associations and they show the flag, literally and figuratively. It makes them a vocal and credible demographic that can and should promote sensible practices.
- Sailors are socially and economically diverse, so they can engage a broad audience.
- Sailors are committed, which results in a strong fraternity of practitioners.
- Sailors are geeks. They love their gear, and are ideal test pilots for new eco-friendly products.
- Sailors are educated. More than 50 percent have at least a college degree, but they keep learning to refine their skills. Therefore, becoming an eco-savvy mariner is just part of the sailing life.
- Sailboats are green machines. Next to a bicycle, they are the most practical and efficient mobility devices conceived by man. That's instant credibility.
- Get the geezers: Industry figures claim that about 74 percent of hard-core practitioners are 35 and older and one might suspect that many of them are retirees. These are healthy, active, and educated people, who have time and passion for boats. Just look how many retirees work as volunteers for the national park system. They are friendly ambassadors for environmental stewardship programs and enhance the pleasure of enjoying the outdoors. It doesn't get any better than this.

Small steps in the right direction

Given the enormity of the problems that await resolution, it's easy to get discouraged. "You have to use common sense and prioritize," Jennifer Thorne Amann, a senior associate at the American Council for an Energy-Efficient Economy's (ACEEE) Buildings Program and co-author of the *Consumer Guide to Home Energy Savings*, told National Geographic magazine. "Don't agonize too much. Think about what you'll be able to sustain . . . If you have trouble reaching your goal in one area, remember there's always something else you can do." It is a useful suggestion. Since sailing means different things to different people, there are many ways to go about making and promoting positive changes. Start with a modest goal and take small steps to make the transition smooth and fun. Evaluate results and make adjustments if necessary. Once you find out what works, encourage others to try it too, and pass the idea on to their sailing buddies. Before long you have your own grass-roots campaign.

Take heart in this story from the Virgin Islands, which I like to share to show what is possible if incremental steps are taken: AKASHA, a crewed 76-foot charter catamaran, with five double cabins for 10 guests, has installed a water chiller filtration system to cut back on plastic bottle use. The crew calculated that this step reduces their boat's trash by 500 empty plastic water bottles per charter. If they do 20 charter trips per season, that would amount to 10,000 fewer bottles to transport, discard or recycle, which is very complicated on an island that doesn't have recycling services. So with one fairly minor change, the AKASHA crew saved raw materials and water, which would be used to make the bottles. Simultaneously, they reduced carbon emissions that would have been created by transporting the bottles from the manufacturer to their boat, and they cut down on landfill matter, because bottles you don't buy won't have to be thrown out. This is the point where I start fantasizing: If 25 charter yachts of similar size decided to do it, the number of bottles saved would be approximately 250,000 over just one season. To illustrate the magnitude of this achievement let's take one more step with this little Fermi problem and lay all these bottles down in a row. With an estimated average bottle height of eight inches (approximately the height of a Nalgene bottle), that row would be 31.5 miles long, roughly covering a distance from Midtown Manhattan to Greenwich, Connecticut. If sailors are as passionate about a healthy environment as they are about sailing, they recognize their role in creating these problems. At the same time, they need to remember that a small change can have big impact if it can be scaled up. This knowledge makes it worthwhile to look for better choices that are available and help mitigate the environmental impact.

Our future, for better or worse, depends on the condition of the planet that we turn over to the generations that follow: Will they be able to enjoy sailing as much as we do? Will they still enjoy the company of dolphins? Will they witness the spectacle of breaching whales? Will they find turtle tracks in the sand? Will they still catch fish or plastic mutants? If we start contemplating the consequences of our actions, not just as sailors but also as responsible citizens and consumers, we have already taken the first and most important step on this journey toward sustainability. But it will take effort, patience and discipline to go the rest of the way, because there won't be instant gratification. What we sow now will be harvested long after we are gone. Only if we don't shrink from responsibility, do our part, and accept the challenge that real change starts with every one of us, do we have a fighting chance to get the good ship Earth sailing on the proper course once again.

More People, More Sailors?

The good news is that the population is still growing so there will be opportunities for our industry to sell new people on the sport," is how Jonathan Banks, managing director of Sail America, encouraged a meeting of industry professionals during the dark times of recession. It is a reasonable assumption from an economic perspective. More people will buy more, but will they be able to sail more, too?

The UN Population Division estimates that the world population will grow from 6.7 billion today to 9.2 billion by 2050. Most of the growth will occur in the developing world, while industrialized nations will remain flat or even decline, with one exception: The U.S. will continue to add people, as it has done since the arrival of the Pilgrims. U.S. population is projected to rise from currently 306 million to approximately 400 million by 2050. If all of them become sailors, the industry is on track to become a juggernaut, but the reality is that few of them will, if the present problems of rising costs and diminishing access to water is any indication. One possible solution could be the concept of shared boat ownership, which has some industry executives worried, because if everybody shares boats, who'll buy them? One possibility is taking the old business model to emerging markets in Asia and Russia that have the potential for big growth. If and when this will happen remains to be seen, because much of that will depend on the world economic climate.

"Everything will be a size smaller than it used to be," said Torsten Conradi, principal at the yacht design firm Judel/Vrolijk &

Co and president of the German association of boat builders. If small should become beautiful again and bringing new people to the sport remains a top goal, as the industry repeatedly states, public sailing clubs will play a more prominent role. Easing people into the sport through a social experience that goes beyond tacks and jibes is not just good for the future, but it has a broad appeal that has blunted the effects of a bad economy. "Membership is up by 20 percent," said Anthony Sandberg, president of the Olympic Circle Sailing Club. The year of 2008, he said, "was the best year in our history." Institutions like OCSC and community sailing centers in many major cities in the U.S. reach out to sailors who don't want to deal with stuffy yacht clubs, high initiation fees, and the costs of ownership. They seem to be on a promising path, growing the sport by making it more affordable—and sustainable. If we can share cars, vacation homes or office space, why not share boats, too? (See fractional ownership in Chapter 13)

To imagine the role of sailing in the future, look at some numbers that illustrate the likely road ahead. When I was born, there were approximately 3 billion people on earth. If I am lucky to live to age 90, to 2051, I could be one of nearly 10 billion world citizens. That's a stunning thought that gets magnified by the implications of the improved standards of living that are sought by the citizens of developing nations who are looking for opportunities in free-market capitalism, so they too can live the American dream, which now is the global dream, owning a car (or two), a home and, perhaps, a boat. Goodlander and other cruisers who have visited remote islands observed that satellite TV is transporting appealing images of a consumption-oriented lifestyle to people who sustain themselves through fishing and agriculture. West Marine founder Randy Repass has noticed it too during his excursions in the South Pacific and put it succinctly: "We want to live like them and they want to live like us." Capitalism has ended poverty for many millions over the last several decades, with many more knocking at the door to affluence. However, if we continue running the operation on this planet they way we have, there won't be enough of anything to go around. Not for 7 billion, let alone for 10 billion if all of them are to have decent standards of living, food and clean water, access to education and health care and all the toys that are so unnecessary, but so much fun. Let history be the guide to the scenario that's likely to happen when the gap between the haves and the have-nots widens.

The curve of consumption

"The world has serious consumption problems, but we can solve them if we choose to do so," wrote Jared Diamond, a professor of geography at the University of California, Los Angeles in a New York Times op-ed piece "What's Your Consumption Factor?" on January 2, 2008. He suggested that "the average rates at which people consume resources like oil and metals, and produce wastes like plastics and greenhouse gases, are about 32 times higher in North America, Western Europe, Japan and Australia than they are in the developing world." Jared believes the real problem is that "each of us 300 million Americans consumes as much as 32 Kenyans. With 10 times the population, the United States consumes 320 times more resources than Kenya does."

The obvious solution is that resources will have to be managed better. Sailors could contribute valuable insight, because going to sea in a small boat requires skills in resource management that are applicable in the larger context. For argument's sake, one could imagine the world as Ark 2.0, which is a self-contained vessel with all living creatures aboard that perpetually sails on a great circle route without stopping to take on more supplies. The challenge is that the number of the one species with the most voracious appetite is increasing. That's "more weight on the rail," but trouble for the galley, because rail meat wants to be fed. Since supplies are limited, all on Ark 2.0 face a tough choice: Keep plundering the larder until it is empty and mutiny breaks out, or find ways to sustain the ship's growing population. There is free and abundant energy from the sun which helps to grow food, create power, and which produces the wind that billows the sails with a nice breeze. Pulling this off is entirely possible if all aboard our factitious vessel are on the same page. Here on Earth, this will require smart leadership with smart policies, smart industries with smart products and smart consumers with smart and sustainable habits.

If the world's population would stop increasing and all other consumption would remain flat, a China that lives like the U.S. "would roughly double world consumption rates. Oil consumption would increase by 106 percent, for instance, and world metal consumption by 94 percent," Jarred surmised. Add India into this mix, and world consumption rates would triple. If the whole developing world would follow, world consumption rates would increase elevenfold. It would be as if the current world population ballooned to 70+ billion people. Hard to imagine that Ark 2.0 could support this kind of demand, so what's going to give? Politicians and industry captains cringe at the notion of cutting consumption, because to them that means cutting profits.

"Nevertheless, whether we get there willingly or not, we shall soon have lower consumption rates, because our present rates are unsustainable," Diamond suggested, adding that, "much of American consumption is wasteful and contributes little or nothing to quality of life."

Some select statistics show why. For the year 2003, the World Research Institute had the U.S. at the top of gasoline consumption with 432 gallons per capita, followed by Canada with 318 GPC, the United Arab Emirates with 264 GPC. France clocked in at 69 GPC, but that number looks skewed since a large percentage of European vehicles run on diesel fuel. The average Chinese consumed only 12 gallons of gasoline in 2003, a quantity that is sure to be higher now. India was near the bottom at 2.6 gallons per individual, a notch above Mozambique and Tanzania with an annual per-capita consumption of 1.6 gallons. Expressed differently, one U.S. citizen consumed on average more than 270 times the amount of gas of one Tanzanian. The annual per-capita electricity consumption for 2004 published in the *CIA World Factbook 2003–2008* has Iceland in the lead with 28,213 kilowatt hours, followed by Norway with 24,645 kWh. The U.S. is ninth with 13,351 kWh, while the average Haitian used only 30.45 kWh of electricity per year, which is one 926th of an Icelander's tally.

To keep all mouths fed and happy aboard Ark 2.0, we must become proficient with the principle of reducing, reusing and recycling. Sustainable fishing, logging and agriculture are not hard to figure out. It's already been done. We know what it takes to reduce carbon emissions, but we can't seem to make it a priority, even though it appears inevitable. Again, sailors are a few steps ahead of the game, because they can get to net-zero, which means producing as much energy as they use. They already tap into renewable energy for propulsion and on-board electricity production. If we start thinking long-term with a more eco-centric focus, transposing the limitations of a sailboat's microcosm to the larger context of our planet's predicament doesn't seem that difficult. If this happens, we might be able to develop and promote solutions that are equitable, scalable and sustainable, all without going out of business.

It seems pretty clear in my opinion that the industrialized world must learn to live well on quite a bit less, so others might live a bit better. And sailing can teach this principle of living simply but living well. "These are desirable trends, not horrible prospects," Diamond said. "In fact, we already know how to encourage the trends; the main thing lacking has been political will."

The cost of fuel

A lack of political will has also kept fuel prices low, which is why GM and other U.S. automakers were able to sell millions of inefficient and heavy vehicles, such as a Hummer, which is favorably rated in the 2008 Fuel Economy Guide at 13 to 16 miles per gallon. Yet, compared to large powerboats that can guzzle 40, 60, 80 gallons or more per hour, a Hummer could be mistaken for an example of fuel efficiency. When a gallon at the fuel dock was $5, people were dismayed and angry, because that's not what they had signed up for. Power boaters were hit harder than sailors, because their mode of propulsion left them no choice and put them at the mercy of politicians, speculators and natural disasters that yank the oil price around. They had to pay up or stay home, while sailors still had the wind. But they too felt the heartburn as they traded a Ben Franklin for 20 gallons of diesel.

It was a taste of what Europeans have to endure and why sailing is so popular over there, where a gallon of gasoline costs at least twice as much as in the U.S., even though the net price of gasoline is less. The difference is in the taxes and the willingness of governments to set price signals that make alternative energy more attractive by keeping fossil fuels expensive. Hence the prominence of solar and wind power in the energy mix and the advances in fuel-cell technology for mobile applications such as RVs and pleasure boats, which will be discussed in the following chapters. Nobody wants to see the $5 gallon return to U.S. fuel docks, yet economists suggest that it may happen again soon.

The option of zero-emission propulsion aside, here are three reasons why I think of sailing as a sustainable insurance against unpredictability and volatility of oil prices:

Demand in emerging economies: As discussed above the majority of the world is trying to catch up to the lifestyle of the industrialized countries and that takes a lot of energy, mostly in the form of fossil fuels such as coal and crude oil. "The coming triple-digit oil prices: most think tanks and government experts predict a price decline in coming decades. They're dead wrong," asserted Philip K. Verleger Jr., principal of PK Verleger LLC in a paper published by International Economy Publications, Inc in 2007. "World energy consumption grew at five percent per year from 1951 to 1970 during a time of profound economic change." History may well repeat itself in the coming decade, Verleger suggested, as China, India, and other nations are moving from developing to developed nations. "Consumption can be expected to increase at a pace close to the rate of economic growth in these nations, just as it did in Europe, Japan, and the United States following the Second World War."

Politics and greed: The spike in gasoline prices in the early 1970s was caused by the decision of the Organization of Petrol Exporting Countries (OPEC) to cut back production, which caused a supply shock and turned oil into a political weapon. The oil price that topped out at $147 a barrel in 2008 was called demand shock, but if demand was outstripping supplies, why no long lines at gas stations? Many, especially outside the U.S., thought that speculation on the future markets drove up prices, which played into the hands of the oil-friendly George W. Bush administration that sought access to the 14 to 16 billion barrels of crude oil that is believed to slumber beneath the outer continental shelf off the U.S. coasts. However, these reserves had been off limits since George H. Bush had implemented an executive ban on additional offshore exploration. "The only way [to get approval from Congress] was to escalate the oil price in the future markets, so people would riot at the pumps and force Congress to lift the ban," the German stockbroker Dirk Müller wrote in his book *Crashcourse*. On July 14, 2008, the president issued a memorandum to lift the executive prohibition, and Congress did exactly that on September 24, 2008. The following drop of crude oil prices by 10 percent, Müller's book suggests, was a direct consequence.

Uncertain economic future: The International Energy Agency predicted the possibility of a supply deficit around the year 2013, citing a drop in oil reserves and the scaled back investments for the development of new oil sources, which still offer plenty of crude, but are technically more difficult and expensive to exploit (i.e. tar sands and offshore wells in deep water). Rising demand and tight resources would combine to push prices to or above $200 per barrel, which would throttle economic growth worldwide.

With so many question marks and uncertainties, it's easy to despair since all of it is beyond an individual's control. If there is one remedy it's this: Cast off and hoist sail.

Climate Change 101

The National Energy Information Center says that levels of greenhouse gases have increased by about 25 percent since large-scale industrialization began around 150 years ago and during the past two decades about 75 percent of anthropogenic emissions came from fossil fuel consumption. Fossil fuels are made up of hydrogen and carbon and account for 85 percent of the primary energy consumed in the United States. When these fuels are burned, the carbon combines with oxygen to yield carbon dioxide, the most ubiquitous greenhouse gas that accumulates in the atmosphere where it traps heat that is radiated back into space from the earth's surface. It's like a giant pressure cooker and we are the frogs that are slowly boiling in it, unable to escape while we keep turning up the heat. Photosynthesis enables the exchange of carbon between land, sea and the atmosphere, so there's carbon in the air, but also absorbed in the oceans and in the landmass (i.e. the forests). Despite this absorption, scientists estimate that we're running a carbon surplus of approximately four billion metric tons that are added to the atmosphere and the oceans annually.

Where is it coming from? About 80 percent of U.S. carbon dioxide emissions are produced by burning coal and petroleum for transportation, power generation and industrial purposes. A number to keep in mind: According to the EPA, burning one gallon of gasoline produces on average 19.4 pounds of CO_2, diesel about 22.2 pounds. The International Energy Agency (IEA) Statistics Division says the average per capital motor gasoline consumption in the U.S. was 426 gallons in 2005, which translates into 3.5 tons of CO_2 generated per person just by driving. That's enough to drive 11,000 miles, if the car gets around 25 miles to the gallon. It also adds more than 8,000 pounds or 3.5 tons of CO_2 to the atmosphere.

Climate change is a complex topic; denial and spin doctoring have clouded the issues for a long time. General Motors Vice Chairman and chief of product development, Bob Lutz, once famously dismissed global warming as a "total crock of shit." Mr. Lutz, who's retired, later said in a blog, "my thoughts on what has or hasn't been the cause of climate change have nothing to do with the decisions I make to advance the cause of General Motors." On April 24, 2009, the New York Times carried a story about the efforts of the Global Climate Coalition, a group that was financed by corporations and interest groups with ties to oil, coal and auto industries. Despite evidence to the contrary, GCC waged an aggressive campaign against the idea that emissions of heat-trapping gases could lead to global warming, asserting that "the role of greenhouse gases in climate change is not well understood." But documents filed in a federal lawsuit show that as far back as 1995, the coalition's scientists had concluded that "the scientific basis for the greenhouse effect and the potential impact of human emissions of greenhouse gases such as CO_2 on climate is well established and cannot be denied."

Environmentalists, the story continues, have compared this tactic to the practices of tobacco companies, which for a long time doubted science that linked cigarette smoking to lung cancer. "By questioning the science on global warming," these environmentalists say, "groups like the Global Climate Coalition were able to sow enough doubt to blunt public concern about a consequential issue and delay government action."

A more sober assessment of climate change is offered by bird populations migrating north at an unprecedented pace and in large numbers, as the Audubon Society found in the annual Christmas Bird Count. Birds are some of the most adaptable creatures on the planet, because they are able to move to find favorable habitat conditions, which makes them sensitive indicators for ecological change, long before it affects humans. What used to be the canary in the coalmine now has become the canary of global warming. Among the most active migrants are seabirds, such as the marbled murrelet and the ring-billed gull, which is also found far inland, mostly around garbage dumps. This bird is well adapted to human presence and has migrated up to 350 miles farther north, but it's also a threat to other species, because it can out-compete them for food and habitat. Another species that moves north is the red-breasted merganser, a magnificent fish-eating duck that winters in saltwater venues, but also on the Great Lakes. The Audubon Society's report concludes that birds "are sending us a powerful signal that we need to 1) take policy action to curb climate change and its impacts, and 2) help wildlife and ecosystems adapt to unavoidable habitat changes, even as we work to curb climate change itself."

Dr. Dee Boersma, a conservation biologist at the University of Washington, has been researching the behavioral patterns of breeding penguins in Punta Tombo, Argentina since 1982. "Through the tagging we've been able to show that in the last decade, the birds are swimming about 25 miles further in search of food," she said in an interview that was published by the New York Times on March 31, 2009. "They're having trouble finding enough fish to eat. That costs a penguin energy and time while their mate is sitting on the egg, starving." These stressed penguins now lay their eggs three days later than a decade ago, which means that chicks are leaving for the sea at the wrong time, i.e. when the fish aren't close to the colony. This increases the death rate, so fewer will return as adults to breed. Since 1987 Boersma recorded a population decline in Punta Tombo's colony of 22 percent caused by scarcity of food, which is a direct consequence of climate change and exploitation of fish stocks, but also by oil pollution that comes from ships. "The big thing is that penguins are showing us that climate change has already happened. The birds are trying to adapt, but evolution is not fast enough to allow them to do that over the long term. If we we're going to have penguins, I think we are going to have to do ocean zoning and try to manage people."

Fingerprinting the causes

With 18 of the warmest years being recorded in the last two decades, global warming is affecting boaters especially in the southeast of the U.S., but also along the Gulf Coast. In the 20th century, the earth's surface warmed by about 1.4 °F, states a report by the Pew Center on Global Climate Change, parts of which are quoted here. This was caused by natural factors such as solar radiation and volcanic activity, but also by the impact of man i.e. by the release of carbon dioxide and methane, two potent greenhouse gasses. As technology has advanced, i.e. with the use of satellite-based measurements, analysis of the CO_2 that's trapped in Arctic and Antarctic ice and more accurate computer models, scientists have been busy revising projections that were made only a few years ago. And most of these revisions are toward the negative. In early 2009, scientific evidence was mounting that Antarctica, which was considered somewhat immune to the global warming trend, was warming up too.

Sailors know about climate variations caused by winds and ocean currents, which scientists call "internal climate variability." Just think of the El Niño and La Niña years that change precipitation patterns and surface temperatures around the Pacific because existing atmospheric heat and moisture are redistributed. Climate change, on the other hand, is the result of an increase of heat through external forcing that fingerprinting models identified as either natural or man-made. While man-made greenhouse gases trap heat in the atmosphere, they boost warming over land more than over oceans, but there are other influences, too. Man also produces aerosols and particulate matter that reflect sunlight back into the atmosphere, which results in localized cooling trends. Then there are natural causes such as the 11-year cycle of solar activity that causes periodic warming in some parts of the atmosphere, while volcanoes, which blow ash into the atmosphere during eruptions, prevent sunlight from reaching the earth's surface and results in a sudden but short-lived cooling.

During the past decades man-made influence on the climate was established by independent modeling of different components in the climate system. Surface warming in the 20th century, for instance, took place in distinct patterns, a warming trend from ca. 1910 to ca. 1940, a moderate cooling from 1940 to ca.1975 and strong warming from 1975 to date. "If not for the temporary cooling trend between 1940 and 1975, from volcanic activity and man-made aerosol emissions, the earth might be even warmer than it is today," the Pew Center stated.

Warmer water, weirder weather

Oceans, as we know, have been warming too. Researchers from the Scripps Institution of Oceanography, Lawrence Livermore National Lab, the National Center of Atmospheric Research, and the Hadley

Center in the UK found in their studies that oceans are warming much faster around the equator, which has direct implications for the proliferation of hurricanes and cyclones. This influences cruising sailors' itineraries, because they will have to travel farther and take more precautions sooner to avoid getting caught up in them. This scenario is very likely to become more frequent in the future. Predictions are getting better, but cannot always pinpoint the exact mix of the ingredients that are combined in the weather kitchen, i.e. the influence of El Niño and La Niña patterns in the Pacific, the intensity of Saharan dust storms on the formation of Atlantic hurricanes, or the position of the Bermuda high-pressure system on the tracks of these storms. There's just one thing we know for sure: There are better years and there are catastrophic years.

BoatU.S. reported that in 2005, one of the most active hurricane years on record with 28 named storms, including the infamous Katrina which laid waste to New Orleans, the recreational boating industry suffered more than $1 billion in hurricane-related losses. Marinas in the hurricane belt have responded to the new realities and taken precautions to prevent or limit storm damage by fortifying their facilities, including surge protection, docks and dry storage stacks. Breakwaters and wave attenuators now must be able to resist big surges and waves. Floating docks need pilings that are tall enough to handle a 12-foot surge and strong enough to withstand large loads. Dry stack barns need to comply with new building codes, so they hold up in winds of 120 knots or more. While these measures offer them peace of mind, boaters also have to face higher marina fees, yacht club dues and insurance rates.

Researchers went deep off the California coast to learn more about how global warming affects the health of the oceans. Early in 2009, they deployed a video camera to a depth of 3,000 feet to add it to the Monterey Accelerated Research Station (MARS), an underwater observatory that studies currents, seismic activity and how higher acidity affects marine life in real time. "With rising sea levels as a result of ocean warming and ice caps melting, we need better observations recorded regularly and openly to better quantify what's happening to the oceans and the planet," the Associated Press quoted John Orcutt, a professor of geophysics at the University of San Diego's Scripps Institution of Oceanography. Oceans absorb most of the CO_2 in the atmosphere, which is a form of natural carbon sequestration. However, CO_2 emissions not only increase the CO_2 content in the ocean, but also its acidity, which harms marine life and especially fragile coral reefs, which are not only habitat to a very diverse population of marine flora and fauna, but also a magnet for charter sailors who flock to exotic destinations to snorkel and dive around these reefs.

Scientists at NASA's Goddard Institute for Space Studies, who have studied the Earth's energy balance with a combination of global climate models, ground-based measurements, and satellite observations, asserted that the climate balance is fragile. Earth absorbs more energy than it is radiating back to space, but some of that excess energy is stored in the oceans, which could mean that some of the impact of global warming is yet to happen.

Although some of it has warmed the land and molten pole ice caps and glaciers, much of this energy imbalance that is parked in the ocean has yet to make its presence felt. Instead, the scientists said that in addition to the warming over the past century, an additional increase in average global temperatures by 1°F (0.6°C) is likely to happen, even if we managed to stop adding to the greenhouse gas concentration and other climate-warming influences immediately. So climate change is already programmed into our future, which means we have to prepare to deal with weird weather that makes dry areas drier and wet areas wetter.

In February 2009, southern Australia suffered through record heat of more than 110°F (43.3 °C) and catastrophic wildfires that devastated whole villages and killed nearly 100 people, while at the same time Queensland on the northeast coast of the continent encountered record rainfall and flooding. In the U.S., record floods in the Midwest are contrasted by a prolonged and more intense drought in the Southwest. "With severe drought from Oklahoma to California, a broad swath of the Southwest is basically robbed of having a sustainable lifestyle," testified Christopher Field of the Carnegie Institution of Science before Congress. He warned that major cities in the western U.S. such as Sacramento, California, could experience heat waves for up to 100 days a year. Other scientists are concerned that the climate predictions made by the Intergovernmental Panel on Climate Change (IPCC) in 2001 fell short, since the effects of greenhouse gasses on the atmosphere are likely to be far stronger than predicted. Hans-Martin Fussel, one of the authors who updated the old IPCC report, commented: "Today, we have to assume that the risks of negative impacts of climate change on humans and nature are larger than just a few years ago."

Sea levels rising

A rising tide lifts all ships. This scenario might become reality on a grander scale than we want, affecting boaters who keep their vessels in or near the water. Warmer temperatures have already taken a heavy toll on sea ice and glaciers. The Arctic ice cap has shrunk to record lows, threatening the habitat of polar bears and opening the North-west Passage for vessel traffic. Based on the IPCC's assumption that global temperatures could rise between 3.6 and 7.2°F (2 to 4°C), ocean levels are bound to rise, but it is hard to come up with exact predictions as to when and how much, because water warms slower than air. But research published in the journal *Climate Dynamics* shows that the ocean's sea level could rise by three feet or more, which is about three times as much as the IPCC predicted just a few years ago. "Instead of making calculations based on what one believes will happen with the melting of the ice sheets we have made calculations based on what has actually happened in the past," said Aslak Grinsted, a geophysicist at the Center for Ice and Climate at the Niels Bohr Institute at the University of Copenhagen. "We have looked at the direct relationship between the global temperature and the sea level 2000 years into the past."

Analysis of ice core samples and growth rings in trees led researchers to calculations of global temperatures over the past two millennia, which they linked to the recorded observations of sea levels that go back approximately 300 years. They found an astonishing variance from the warmer period around the 12th century when the sea level was approximately 8 inches (20 cm) higher than today, to the 18th century when temperatures were cooler and sea levels were 10 inches (25 cm) lower than today. Assuming that the climate in the coming century could be 5.4°F (3°C) warmer, the sea level could rise by 3 to 4 feet. For this to occur, ice sheets will have to melt much faster than previously thought. At the end of the last ice age, ca. 12,000 years ago, ice sheets melted so quickly that the sea level rose 0.4 inch (11 millimeters) per year or more than three feet in a century.

Is it possible to recreate these conditions? Grinsted believes that it is, and other research indicates that it already is happening. On April 28, 2009, Reuters reported that an area of an Antarctic ice shelf that covered 270 square miles of ice—bigger than Singapore or Bahrain and almost the size of New York City—had broken into icebergs after the collapse of an ice bridge. It was the latest of about 10 shelves on the Antarctic Peninsula to retreat in a trend linked by the U.N. Climate Panel to global warming.

Temperatures on the Antarctic Peninsula have warmed by up to 5.4°F (3°C) this century, according to David Vaughan, a British Antarctic Survey scientist. It reflects a trend that climate scientists blame on global warming from burning fossil fuels in cars, factories and power plants. The Wilkins Shelf has already shrunk by about a third from its original size of 6,200 square miles (16,000 square kilometers) when first spotted decades ago. The good news: Because ice shelves already float in the water, their melting has less impact on the sea level than melting glaciers, which tumble into the ocean from land.

Things aren't looking any better on the other end of the globe, in the Arctic, where a fast and steady decline of the sea ice is being recorded. Some scientists believe that the Arctic could lose all its summer ice as early as 2015. Data released by the National Snow and Ice Data Center and NASA show that the extent of winter sea ice in 2008-2009 was among the lowest on record, with the past six years all setting records for maximum lows. Because of this change, officials were pushing for the passing of the Law of the Sea Treaty to regulate expanding and changing human activity in the Arctic, like shipping, oil exploration and fishing. The loss of sea ice in the Arctic may be more dramatic than scientists originally thought, "There's already impacts, in terms of the climate, in terms of the people," the Washington Post quoted Walt Meier, a scientist with the NSIDC.

At this rate of warming, how long until the effects will be felt by the average sailor? A 2009 multi-agency report, titled "Coastal Sensitivity to Sea-Level Rise: A Focus on the Mid-Atlantic Region," examined how to plan for and adapt to rising sea levels. Led by the EPA with contributions by the USGS and NOAA, the report pointed out how sea-level rise can affect coastal communities and habitats, i.e. by submerging low-lying lands, beach erosion, converting wetlands to open water, more intense coastal flooding, and higher salinity of estuaries and freshwater aquifers. The report cited natural and human-induced factors that can vary by region and found that some stretches of U.S. coast are already affected. The Mid-Atlantic region was considered one of the areas in the U.S. that is likely to see the greatest impacts from rising waters, coastal storms, and a high concentration of population near the water. Taking a cue from hurricane-proofing efforts along Florida's coasts, it will most likely result in higher marina fees and insurance payments to help offset the improvements of infrastructure. Even passing storms could have more extreme consequences if storm surge overwhelms the outer islands and lower jetties and breakwaters that used to offer enough protection in the past. Drysailing and keeping the vessel on a trailer on higher ground looks like a viable tactic to escape the worst of problems caused by storm surge.

Loss of biodiversity

What do polar bears, hippos, nurse sharks, and black-tailed godwits have in common? They have joined the Red List of Threatened Species, published by the International Union for the Conservation of Nature and Natural Resources (IUCN), which names more than 16,000 others, too. The IUCN says loss of biodiversity is increasing despite a global convention committing governments to stem it. "The 2006 Red List shows a clear trend; biodiversity loss is increasing, not slowing down," IUCN director-general Achim Steiner told the BBC News Web site in 2006. "The implications of this trend for the productivity and resilience of ecosystems and the lives and livelihoods of billions of people who depend on them are far-reaching."

Most of the problems are caused by human activities, such as habitat loss, climate change, import of non-native species, over-exploitation and pollution.

"There's no question that we are in a mass extinction spasm right now," said David Wake, professor of integrative biology at UC Berkeley in an interview published by Global Research. "Amphibians have been around for about 250 million years. They made it through when the dinosaurs didn't. The fact that they're cutting out now should be a lesson for us." But that's not all.

The more species are assessed, the more are considered endangered. Jean-Christophe Vie, deputy coordinator of IUCNs species program, told the BBC, adding that "16,000 is a massive underestimate of the true problem." Polar bears are listed as vulnerable to extinction based on forecasts that their population might get completely wiped out within the next 100 years. Loss of Arctic ice means loss of hunting grounds and shortage of food. But political circumstances also can victimize animals such as the hippopotamus, which suffered a 95-percent decline within the last decade in the Democratic Republic of Congo, according to the IUCN. The country's turbulent political situation permitted unregulated hippo hunting for meat and ivory in their teeth.

In the ocean, sharks are disappearing at an unprecedented rate, because they are hunted for their fins, are killed by driftnets or end up as by-catch. As fisheries extend into deeper, largely unregulated waters, many more species could be on the verge of a sharp decline. "The desperate situation of many sharks and rays is just the tip of the iceberg," said Craig Hilton-Taylor of the IUCN Red List Unit. He urged action to improve management practices and implement conservation measures before it is too late.

While last-ditch preservation efforts have had limited success and the number of the species on this list is relatively stable, biodiversity continues to decline, despite the UN Biodiversity Convention, which demands from governments that they halt the trend by 2010.

"Restoring lost biodiversity within our lifetime is an illusion, but by changing our ways we can at least stop making it worse, perhaps even avert the specter of catastrophic bio collapse," says Peter Raven, past President of the American Association for the Advancement of Science, in the foreword to the AAAS Atlas of Population and Environment.

There is a silver lining on the horizon, though. Numerous nonprofit organizations use sailing as an educational tool for adults and students to build awareness for the importance of marine conservation and healthy oceans, which impact the lives of every human on this planet, not just in coastal regions. "Sailing is the proper vehicle to get our message across," said Dave Robinson, director of SeaLife Conservation in Santa Cruz, California. "Up to 40 percent of our guests have never sailed before. People's eyes open when the engine is shut off. You could deliver the message in a classroom, but nothing has the powerful impact of a sailboat on the ocean, as part of the marine environment."

Deliberations of Design

Sustainability as a catchword for efficiency means getting more with less. More performance with the same energy or same performance with less power. That's a good start and favors sailboats and bicycles, two of the simplest and most efficient means of transportation conceived by man. By contrast, propulsive power derived from internal combustion looks very wasteful. If a 180-pound person chose to drive a 6,000-pound vehicle 2.5 miles to the grocery store and back to get a loaf of bread and a quart of milk, the vehicle weight eclipses the weight of the driver, plus the payload more than 30 times.

Moving so much weight requires a sizeable engine that probably burns in excess of half a gallon for a 5-mile roundtrip on city streets. If burning one gallon of gasoline produces on average 19.4 pounds of CO_2, as the EPA suggests, that 5-mile round-trip would equal tailpipe emissions of nearly 10 pounds. On the other hand, if that same 180-pound person took a 20-pound bicycle and a backpack and did the same trip on pedal power, the equation changes dramatically, because the vehicle weight now is only a little more than one tenth of the payload and the rider's weight. So in this case, the bike wins the sustainability battle hands down. Besides sparing the air, it also provides the collateral benefit of a good workout, and some potential time savings if the cars are gridlocked. Sure, but what good is a bicycle for towing a boat? The only answer I can offer is that in an ideal world, we'd have the right wheels for each job. And often times we do, we just are not aware of it, or we don't care to make that switch. I drive an old battered truck that hauls a boat or dirt for the garden. It gets less than stellar gas mileage, but I try to take the bike and/or public transport whenever I have only minor cargo to haul around town, which happens surprisingly often. I used this example to illustrate weight consciousness as a subset of sustainable thinking. And that's where boats and bicycles are very similar. Lighter is better and more efficient, because it takes less energy to move and that means you go faster or you go farther. Not a bad set of alternatives, if you ask me.

Looking at fast and efficient sailing craft like the A-class catamarans (LOA 18 feet, weight ca. 150 lbs), or the International Moth (LOA 11 feet, weight ca. 60 lbs), lightness is not the only key attribute for speed. Slender hulls and minimal wetted surface are important too. The moth uses hydrofoils at the bottom of the centerboard and the rudder blade to ride above the water.

Photo 4.1 Riding high and (nearly) dry: A foiler moth is a small dinghy on hydrofoils. Less wetted surface means less resistance and blistering speed. *Bladerider/Virginia Veal*

Both the A-class catamaran and the foiler moths are so efficient that they need neither jibs nor spinnakers to achieve speeds in excess of 20 knots. Looking at these boats, it's also hard to miss how modern boats benefited from new technology and construction materials that are light and strong. The flipside is that pushing the envelope and achieving efficiency at all costs leads to extreme boats that have limited appeal for mainstream customers and can intimidate beginners.

Modern cruising boats also have evolved with new technologies and materials that produce lighter and stiffer hulls. But that's not necessarily a net gain, because of the tendency to stuff boats with a ton of gear, literally and figuratively, especially electronics and conveniences such as hot pressurized water, air conditioning, or refrigeration that make boats infinitely more complex and require large and heavy battery banks and often a generator to provide the power, plus cables, inverters etc. I always think of the video "The Story of Stuff," when I get on such a boat, from wine coolers to electric adjustments of the backrest angle in the queen-size bunk in the owner's cabin.

"The clients' expectation makes it difficult," said Dave Renouf, who handles sales and marketing at Corsair Marine, a builder of trailerable trimarans about to start production of a 50-foot cruising catamaran. "What do you need to put on a boat? The more [stuff] you put on, the more weight you have, the more difficult it is to be efficient. Super light construction with carbon fiber and Kevlar is more expensive." But that's what Corsair decided to use along with resin-infusion techniques and light interior with honeycomb panels covered with veneer. Other equipment details that point toward better efficiency include heat-insulating laminate windows, vacuum-panel insulation for the refrigerator, passive ventilation, and LED lights. A fully kitted-out version of this boat will be pushing seven figures, but it will have all the amenities *and* refreshing performance.

Buy a light boat and load it down with lots of gear and you give up most or all of the gains. It's like following rigorous exercise with a trip to the pastry shop. New technology can do a lot but only goes so far, because the laws of physics refuse to change.

"Reduce the drag below, increase the lift above," is the short and comprehensive explanation offered by naval architect Tom Wylie, who specializes in slender, slippery hull designs that only need one sail. He's not your mainstream designer, but that actually works out to his advantage, since his designs are for simple, light-to-moderate displacement boats with easy handling. But there are collateral benefits too, that translate into a more sustainable boat: Light and easily driven hulls need smaller auxiliary engines that are more fuel-efficient; they are fit to use alternative propulsion technologies such as electric, diesel-electric and hybrid systems; they can be fitted with smaller, more efficient autopilots which draw less power; less power means smaller batteries, which means less weight and a chance to cover more energy needs with solar panels and a wind generator.

"Yachting is as much about popularity as the movie box office and tastes are as ephemeral as the hemlines at a Paris fashion show," Wylie joked. "It changes every year." In a society that emphasizes individuality and freedom of choice, we all want to be different, yet end up looking and behaving just exactly like the next guy. "Efficiency is about science, not fashion, " Wylie pointed out. "It's about physics and focus. Remember Kitty Hawk 1903? We only tend to see the first flight that lasted all of 12 seconds and covered 120 feet, but the bigger lesson was about putting energy on wings." And this crossover relationship has held Wylie's attention, because lift, the force that keeps a plane aloft, also makes a sailboat move. Wyliecat rigs are made of carbon fiber, use a wishbone boom like on a windsurfer and do not have stays. Sail trim needs but three lines: A mainsheet, a vang (called choker) and a downhaul. When the sail is doused, it simply drops into the oval of the wishbone where it is caught by lines that are loosely strung from side to side. So it is simple, light, and cost-effective. These rigs have been around for a long time, i.e. on the New-England style catboats. Even Capt. Nathanael Herreshoff, the consummate innovator, experimented with them. In the late 1970s George Hinterhoeller, who designed the Shark 24 and was part of the first incarnation of C&C Yachts in Canada, used an aluminum version of the wishbone rig for his Nonsuch catboats. Wylie picked it up in the early 1990s, stuck with it, and perfected it by using carbon fiber. "Una-rigs have been shunned by mainstream boat builders and designers," he explained. "But if you look at iceboats, windsurfers, catamarans, etc. you'll see that [these rigs] are as efficient as they are simple, and they're also good for motorsailing." But Wylie goes a couple of steps further: "If you need to buy less, you need to replace less. If you replace less, you throw away less. Just think of the savings on rigging wire and the old used-up sails." His point: Reduce. And still be fat and happy and fast.

Simple boats also get used more. As the skipper of a Wyliecat 39 that was owned by the company I worked for, I saw the sustainability of the KISS principle at work. The boat was ready to go in a couple of minutes. Because it only had one sail, it did not require a large crew. And because there was little that could break, it spent its time sailing, not holding up dock lines. The engine was only used to get in and out of the slip. More than 300 people came along for a ride within the first year, most of them non-sailors and repeat guests. Aside from having a good time, these guests also talked about it, so the boat also produced a great deal of positive vibes for the company—entirely free. This idea was a winner because it produced winners: The guests who had a good time; the owner because he set a great example for company R&R; human resources because people wanted to come work for a company that offered sailboat rides

Photo 4.2 The Tom Wylie-designed DEREK M BAYLIS is a unique and eco-friendly research vessel, operated by Sealife Conservation, a non-profit organization. *Dieter Loibner*

as an employee perk; and sailing itself, because these trips introduced the sport to young and upwardly mobile people who were
looking for cool and fun ways to spend their discretionary income.
That's what I call collateral benefits of sustainability.

SOURCES:
Corsair Marine: www.corsairmarine.com
Wyliecat: www.wyliecat.com

Lighten the load

Regardless of design, a lighter boat is a more efficient boat and
often there is a low-tech solution: Scuttle what you don't need.
Barter or trade for what you need by giving away what you can do
without. But there is also a technical aspect to lightening the load
and improving the performance of a vintage boat. Replacing the
old aluminum stick with one made from carbon fiber will shave
off some serious weight where it hurts the most, high above the
waterline. "Upgrading to carbon is the cheapest way to a new
boat," Will Rogers from GMT composites, said. "Carbon masts
reduce weight aloft and lower a boat's center of gravity, which
translates into less heel, better pointing and less hobbyhorsing."
There are other benefits, too, like an increased ability to carry
more sail longer, which means fewer trips forward for sail changes
or reefing. And it goes back to the same basic idea: A boat that sails
better sails longer and needs less fuel. "Carbon is becoming pretty
normal as an upgrade for boats that have lost their old rigs," said
Ben Hall, of Hall Spars.

Carbon masts have come a long way since the early days in the
1990s, because construction is better understood. It still is quite
complex and often uses fibers of different moduli that are pre-
impregnated with resin. This material can be braided, wound or
laminated in an open mold in two halves, which are joined later.
Another technique uses dry fibers to which resin is added during the
manufacturing process through vacuum-assisted resin transfer
molding or by brushing on the resin. In general, though, carbon
needs to be laid out in different angles that follow the direction of
the expected load paths. "Carbon is the best material to stand up to
fatigue," explained Ted Van Dusen who makes rowing shells and

unstayed carbon masts. He argues that it can withstand cycling stresses of 65 up to 80 percent of its braking load, compared to only about 20 percent that would be typical for metals. The strength of the laminate determines the load-bearing ability, so good craftsmanship (i.e. backing of holes for fittings) is necessary. What about cost? "Going carbon is less expensive than you'd think," asserted Dave Eck at Forte Carbon Fiber Products in Ledyard, Connecticut. "It begins to make sense for refits."

One customer who has gone the carbon route to upgrade a vintage boat is Louis Meyer, who put such a stick on his 1967 Hinckley Pilot, STRUMMER, and promptly won his class at the Marion-Bermuda Race and took second in the 2007 Bermuda 1-2. "I got a better boat with a kinder motion, and I reef much later," he confirmed the benefits of using a lighter mast. Costs will vary by boat size, but in general range from ca. $16,000 for an unstayed and simple Nonsuch 30 mast to ca. $35,000 for a Swan 44. Depending on the type of fiber and laminate, these numbers can go up considerably, especially when the upgrade extends below the waterline to a new keel and a new rudder.

Photo 4.3 Braiding of a carbon mast profile. *Forte Carbon Fiber Products*

The weight savings could be substantially reduced by heavy stainless-steel standing rigging and mast fittings. One possible solution is replacing old and heavy wires with rod rigging or extremely light and strong synthetic fibers such as PBO, which carry another benefit because they eliminate corrosion and electrolysis. However, UV protection is an issue with synthetic line and not all types will work for all applications, so consulting with a rigging expert should be the first step before committing to a rigging upgrade. Depending on the extremes owners are willing to push (and pay for), carbon masts on mid-size cruisers can save between 100 and 260 pounds, which improves the righting moment and translates into a stiffer boat, more sail-carrying ability and better overall performance. Another aspect is increased safety because of the need for fewer sail changes, which could be an argument for cruising couples or sailors who are often short- or single-handing their boat. A carbon spar is a path to a faster, better sailing boat that still sails when others have to resort to fossil-fuel propulsion. A few tips for avoiding a botched project: Do your homework and get references from sailors who already made the plunge. Check out a boat like yours that has a carbon stick and see if you like how it feels under sail. Get several bids from different manufacturers.

SOURCES:
GMT Composites: www.gmtcomposites.com
Forte Carbon Fiber Products: www.forterts.com
Hall Spars: www.hallspars.com
Novis Composites: www.noviscomposites.com
Southern Spars/Rig Pro: www.southernspars.com

The proper prop

Many sailboats motor quite a bit, which means that the source of propulsion is a gasoline- or diesel engine and the transmitter of this power is a propeller at the end of a straight shaft, a saildrive or an outboard. At any rate, if the propeller has to stay in the water while the boat sails, it creates drag, thus becoming a hindrance to progress. I distinctly remember a test sail on a Fountaine Pajot Eleuthera, a 60-foot catamaran off Miami. The breeze was cranking from the southeast and the boat, which was in light-displacement mode, skipped along on a reach. The crew on board consisted of Fountaine Pajot boss Eric Bruneel, a record setting multihull skipper and winner of the Singlehanded Transatlantic Race, and Philippe Guillemin, another seasoned bluewater racer. The boat was under screecher and hustling along in the low-double digits, nudging 15 knots in the surf passages with both engine in neutral so the fixed-propellers could spin empty to reduce the draft. "That's not bad, considering that we are hauling two big buckets under the boat," Bruneel said in allusion to the props that were holding us back from going even faster. I asked him how much better we could do if these props were folded and he estimated 1.5 to 2 knots, or roughly 10 percent.

Installing a propeller that automatically folds the blades when the shaft doesn't turn to expose a minuscule area to the water when the boat is sailing, "is the single most effective measure to lower drag and increase speed and efficiency," said Chuck Angle, general manager of Flex-O-Fold Propellers North America. "On average you can expect a 10-percent gain in light air, less in blustery conditions."

At one point or another, boat owners with an inboard auxiliary engine are faced with the decision about their prop. As with most equipment decisions, their choice of product is dictated by the kind of sailing they mostly do.

There are several propeller types to consider: Fixed-blade props, which is most common and standard equipment on many cruising boats, feathering and folding. Daysailors won't suffer too badly from a fixed-blade model, as long as their performance requirements under sail rank behind durability, convenience and price. But racers, who are looking to eke out the last ounce of performance from their boat under all circumstances, want to reduce unnecessary drag and most often go with a folding prop. Long-distance cruisers too are candidates for folding props, because an increase of boat speed by three quarters of a knot adds up on long passages. Consider a 20-day voyage that covers 3,000 miles. That's 150 miles a day on average, not unheard of for a mid-sized cruising boat that is reasonably well sailed in the Trades at an average of 6.25 knots. Bump up the average by three quarters of a knot to 7 knots, and the daily distance would increase to 168 miles, which would cover the 3,000 miles in about 17 days. That could mean two days less of gasoline, water and supplies, which further lightens the load and improves efficiency of the vessel. It is a theoretical example, but it illustrates how initially small gains scale up pretty quickly.

A simpler alternative to reduce drag is a feathering prop that aligns the blades to offer less resistance to the current created by the boat's forward motion. It is a viable concept that has been in use for many years, but it does not yield quite the low-drag efficiency of a folding prop. In some cases however, especially older boats with long keels where the prop is close to the stern and requires a cut-out in the rudder blade, they might be the only alternative to a fixed-blade propeller.

But there is another type of propeller that claims to be more efficient. This is the variable-pitch propeller that "senses" the engine load and adjusts the propeller's pitch accordingly. What is it good for? As engine loads vary, so should the pitch of the propeller. It's a little bit like shifting gears in a car. So the efficiency comes from constant operation at the optimum pitch setting, accompanied by better speeds and increased tank range. One manufacturer of self-pitching propellers promises "more thrust at any given engine speed, ahead or astern." For motorsailing, the company explains, "the propeller adopts a coarse pitch setting by taking into account the driving force of the sails. This results in increased speed at very low engine revolutions." Other advertised benefits include more engine revolutions in adverse conditions and better thrust during down-speed maneuvering in port, especially in reverse.

How do you find the proper prop for your boat? Talk to a technician and bring your boat's measurement certificate or the designer's specifications, Chuck Angle recommended. "The factors that are important for sizing the prop are engine rpm, maximum horsepower, displacement of the vessel and the reduction-gear ratio." Steer clear of props that require lubrication, he warned, "cleaning should be enough." Easily driven boats, such as catamarans and racing yachts can increase the pitch by one or two inches, but users must take care to avoid "over-propping." One of the most common mistakes is not getting the numbers right, Angle pointed out, especially the gear ratio. This can be tricky because you need to check the plate on the transmission to get the correct number. Even if you are sure of yourself, asking more questions upfront wouldn't be a bad idea anyway, because it could help avoid paying more later.

But pay you will: Folding propellers are marvels of engineering, made from a nickel-bronze-aluminum alloy, ranging in price from ca. $900 to $3,000 or more, depending on size.

Propellers on sailboats always represent a compromise. Ideally, one would want them to disappear, so they won't create drag when the boat is sailed. On the other hand, when the engine is on, they are supposed to deliver the best thrust and maximum fuel efficiency. Small-boat sailors who use an outboard on a movable bracket won't have to worry about low-drag props. Kill the engine, pull it up, tilt it, and secure it with the shaft well clear of the water. But for others, Angle has some consoling words: "The advantage of low-drag props is that people become sailors again. That's where most of the savings lie. You sail your boat more, you are less prone to start the engine."

SOURCES:
Flex-O-Fold: www.flexofold.com
Variprop: www.varipropusa.com
Autoprop: www.autoprop.com
Maxprop: www.max-prop.com
Gori Propeller: www.gori-propeller.dk

Sustainable from scratch

Yachts that are designed and constructed for sustainable operation are custom jobs that often include considerable luxuries and start with a blank sheet of paper, which in this day and age might be the greatest luxury of them all. Yet there are ways to incorporate off-the-shelf technology in the design process, something that will become more important as raw materials for boat construction become more expensive and disposal of waste will be subject to tighter regulations. Sparkman & Stephens, the venerable New York design firm, was called upon to design SAFIRA, a 129-foot expedition style motor yacht. The brief called for a small carbon footprint to be achieved with subtle and incremental improvements across the board, from furniture and cabin layout to the treatment of wastewater and exhaust fumes. The specifications were not all cast in stone, but the following description should provide a sense for some of the ideas that went into this inconspicuous-looking power yacht.

"My wife and I believe climate change is happening through

global warming, [which is] caused by greenhouse gas emissions from human activity," said SAFIRA's owner, Anthony Bakker, a software executive. "We want to reduce, recycle, and reuse whenever possible and live in a more sustainable, environmentally sensitive way." SAFIRA, Bakker said, should be a showcase for the application of best practices and smart technology, an example for sensible design. And all this without sailing? An expedition style motor yacht, Bakker explained, is the right vessel for his cruising needs, but admitted that omitting wind power "may sound hypocritical to some." At the time we talked he was undecided about adding a kite system or some sort of auxiliary headsail on the forward mast to get some zero-emission propulsion.

Guided by the requirements of Green Star and Leadership in Energy and Environmental Design (LEED), the yacht has bigger windows, ports, skylights and deck prisms that help cut back the number and size of light fixtures, because they admit more ambient light into the interior. Double-pane glass on the exterior windows with energy-efficient and UV-resistant coating minimizes the heating effect of direct sunlight. To reduce heat absorption from sunlight on the aluminum superstructure, it is coated with a low-solar absorption paint. It is a form of passive solar design combined with weatherization, i.e. insulating pipes, walls and floors, weather stripping and sealing doors and windows to reduce the need for heating or cooling. To minimize direct and indirect energy consumption, the interior lighting system uses fiber-optic technology, light-emitting diode (LED) lamps, Xenon bulbs, occupancy sensors and dimmers.

SAFIRA's interior features organic, natural, recycled, sustainable and renewable materials. Wood had to be certified by the Forest Stewardship Council, (EcoTimber or equivalent), paints, finishes and adhesives had to emit either low or no amounts of volatile organic compounds (VOC) and carpets had to be from natural wool, organic cotton or equivalent materials. Wherever possible, horizontal surfaces, plumbing hardware and fittings were made from recycled material like glass (e.g. IceStone, EnviroGlass), paper (PaperStone), concrete (ConcreteWorks, Sonoma Stone) and aluminum (Eleek).

Renewable energy sources like wind and solar supplement the power needs of the house loads, including hot water. Energy-recovery ventilation regulates interior temperature and humidity, while engine rooms, kitchen hood, and bathrooms are vented outboards. Appliances are Energy-Star rated and separate battery banks handle peak energy demand. Provisions were made for the treatment of exhaust with a soot burn-off system and filter, and a recycling system was installed to treat black and gray water. Potable water comes from a low-energy watermaker. In the end, it's all about more efficiency, which translates into less thirst for power, which in turn shrinks the size of the generators, the fuel bill, and the carbon emissions.

Sparkman & Stephens stated that each element in itself might not provide spectacular advantages, but that taken together these incremental improvements measurably improve efficiency and sustainability compared to conventional yachts of similar size and purpose. Personally, I have a hard time endorsing a 370-ton, 130-foot motor yacht that bunkers 17,000 gallons of fuel as an example for sustainability, but I made an effort to peek outside my own little box and found the eco-centric approach in SAFIRA's design worthy of inclusion since it offers ideas that are applicable to sailboats, too. Kudos to the owner, Sparkman & Stephens, and builder Newcastle Shipyards (www.newcastleyacht.com) in Florida for rolling up the sleeves and doing it. If a power yacht can be made green, it ought to be a cinch for any sailboat.

SOURCES:
Sparkman & Stephens: www.sparkmanstephens.com
Newcastle Shipyards: www.newcastleyacht.com
Dragonfly Water Treatment Systems (wastewater treatment):
    www.marinedragonfly.com
Awlgrip (Low Solar Absorption paint): www.awlgrip.com
Hug Engineering (exhaust filter system): www.hug-eng.ch
Furnature (organic cotton, linen, furniture): www.furnature.com
Green Star: www.greenstarinc.org
Lopolight (exterior lighting): www.lopolight.com
Schottel GmbH Propulsion Systems (pod drives): www.schottel.de
SLCE Watermakers: www.slce.net
U.S. Green Building Council: www.usgbc.org
Xenon Architectural Lighting (interior lighting): www.xal.com

What else is outside the box?

If efficiency is one attribute of sustainability, portability and utility are the others. Owning a boat that is tied to the same slip in the same harbor all the time might be OK for some, but one of the true thrills of sailing is taking the craft on the road to explore different venues. This points to small and trailerable boats, which most of us have enjoyed during our earliest years of sailing. My own history includes dinghy and catamaran sailing all over Europe and introduced me to other cultures and venues. The old fishing vessels that used lateen rigs and the power of oar to get to the fishing grounds and haul the catch back to the market where it was sold fresh the next morning. The elegant Skerry cruisers in Scandinavia, thin as a needle and fast as a rocket, designed to excel in the deep waters around the rocky coast of Sweden. Or the Dutch Botter yachts and the German Zeesen, both ancient designs with sideboards that were conceived as working and fishing vessels in coastal areas or on inland waters, where only shallow-draft vessels find unimpeded passage. Form always followed function, nearly to a fault. Efficiency often was found in the delicate compromise between multiple purposes, such as seaworthiness, load-carrying capability and comfort for the crew to live aboard.

Today in this specialized world where performance and thrill reign supreme, it is a lot more difficult to find multi-purpose vessels, especially pleasure boats. Cruising boats surely qualify as floating homes and family transport, sometimes also as charter vessels. Smaller pleasure craft, such as fast catamarans and dinghies, are pretty singular in their mission (and often also really effective), but try to go fishing on a foiler moth.

Yet, they still exist, these multi-purpose sailing craft, even though they might be called exotic by traditionalists. I'd even call them hybrids, because they are suitable for various modes of propulsion and can be operated in different configurations, which broadens their appeal. They are also car-topable, for ultimate portability and they can be stored in the garage or the basement. Another term that comes to mind is "personal sailing craft."

Hobie Cat, one of the more iconic U.S. boat companies, has put several generations of sailors on the water with their sailing catamarans, a trend that has slowed considerably, but still continues with their best-selling Hobie 16 and the Hobie Tiger Formula 18 high-performance cat. In recent years, the firm has focused on the leisure market and has had success with their kayaks, because they are not just paddleboats but also pedalboats.

At the center is the so-called Mirage-Drive, an ingenious system of flippers that extend under the hull of the boat and are pedal-operated. At first, traditional kayakers smirked at the pedal boat concept. But it quickly caught on with less expert paddlers, because legs are stronger than arms and pedaling is a known motion from riding bicycles, so newcomers don't have to learn different paddle stroke techniques or strengthen their upper body muscles. Another benefit is the hands-free operation, so fishing, snapping pictures or holding a beverage does not require a Houdini act. The Hobie Mirage Adventure Island is a 16-foot trimaran that started out as a kayak, but grew two amas which turned it into a "sailyak." You still have the pedal drive and—almost an afterthought—a common paddle. Hobie calls it "a unique sailing machine unlike any other sailing craft on the water." The simple sail plan can be managed from the cockpit by pulling one line. The two amas can be retracted for docking and on-shore transport. Under sail, the flippers of the Mirage Drive are flat against the hull, but when the breeze shuts off, they spring to life. All you do is furl the sail and start pedaling for the barn. The boat also has a daggerboard for better upwind performance and a rudder. Then there is the upgrade path: If you already own the center hull (which is the Hobie Adventure sit-on-top kayak) you can purchase the accessories to make it a sailboat, although stitching it together costs more than buying the complete boat. There are several sustainable ideas here: The craft is small, and at 115 pounds light enough to be carried by two adults. It is car topable, stows in the garage and converts from kayak to sailboat and back to kayak in no time, so it has multi-user appeal. For around $3,500, this little rotomolded yacht has a wide range of uses, as family entertainment on the beach, as a versatile tender on a larger boat and as a water toy in vacation resorts.

The Triak is another personal sailing craft with hybrid qualities that allow the near instantaneous switch from paddling to sailing and vice versa. The Triak is longer (17 feet 9 inches) but lighter (95 pounds) than Hobie's Mirage Adventure Island and has more of a sailboat's feel with approximately 450 pounds of storage space under

Photo 4.4 A true hybrid without question is the Triak sailing kayak. Amas with hydrofoils increase the stability for operation under sail and paddle. *Triak Sports*

the foredeck, and a performance rig that is stepped or folded down from the cockpit, with the pull of a line. A 10-foot crossbeam is fastened behind the cockpit of the center hull and has two small hydrofoiling amas at each end. The Triak was invented by Charlton Bullock, who is British and emigrated to Canada many years ago to build International 14 dinghies, but somehow ended up in the sea-kayaking Mecca of British Columbia. There he tried to fuse sailing and kayaking and by 1994 he was building and selling the Ur-Triaks before relocating to the sunnier climes of Southern California where he continued to refine the design. To show his confidence in the vessel, Bullock took a Triak around Vancouver Island in British Columbia, Canada and down the Gulf of California from San Felipe to La Paz in Baja, Mexico.

The most distinctive feature is the rig which consists of an aluminum bipod mast and boom, plus all the relevant control lines and cleats. The North Sails on the boat I tested included a 40 square-foot lateen-style main with one full batten and a gennaker of the same size that was set from a small bowsprit. The boat is launched with mast down and can be paddled into deeper water, away from the dock. With the amas, the Triak is so stable at rest that an adult can stand up without any problems. After stowing the paddle behind the cockpit, a short pull on the boom unfolds the rig and sets the sail in one fluid motion. Cleating a line is all that's needed. The boat wants to be sailed very much like a beach cat, both upwind and downwind. With a little practice and the gennaker flying, double-digit speeds are attainable on a reach in 12-15 knots of wind and flat water.

As much fun as it was to sail the boat, it didn't take off with consumers, at least initially. Perhaps the price point of $7,500 was a deterrent to some buyers, who might not have appreciated the labor-intensive polyester sandwich construction and features like foam-filled amas and shaped hydrofoils, which help sail the boat upright. But the company is still around and is working on some new models with renowned multihull designers Morelli & Melvin and is looking for a new builder.

As a hardcore dinghy and catamaran sailor I was quite apprehensive about these "unsailboats," but once I started messing about with them, they opened my eyes. Either way, these little hybrids have multiple talents and match the mix of sustainability criteria quite well, which also makes them feasible as cross-over boats that can satisfy different tastes of waterborne fun, or as accessories on larger boats that can be splashed without a lot of fanfare once the hook is down and the kids need therapy for stir craziness.

SOURCES:
Hobie Cat: www.hobiecat.com
Triak Sports: www.triaksports.com

Fossil-fuel Propulsion

Getting in and out of crowded harbors, getting to the starting line, getting home in time for dinner, getting on with it when the breeze shuts off, there's always a reason to douse the sails and turn the key. For most sailors this means firing up a small diesel or an outboard and let King Carbon take over from Mother Nature as source of propulsive energy. While progress is being made with alternative propulsion technologies (see Chapter 7), the reality still is internal combustion and it won't go away anytime soon. But the days of dirty are coming to an end here too, as the burning of fossil fuels is becoming more efficient and less polluting. The legacy of blue smoke and oil sheens is fading, not as quickly as possible, but hopefully still in time.

New technology is trickling down from the automotive world at an accelerated pace: Catalytic converters to filter carbon monoxide in gas engines, common-rail injection technology and computerized fuel injection for diesel engines are just three examples. Boating under steam will be cleaner, but it will require pricey technology. This worries lobbyists and industry representatives, who want to keep equipment costs down and profits up and express concerns about more possible job losses.

However, as the example of the U.S. car industry shows, building large and inefficient vehicles led to "econocide" when gas prices increased, a recession hit, and the political wind changed.

When the House narrowly passed legislation to address global warming and climate change on June 26, 2009, it was the first time that either house of Congress had approved a bill to curb emission of heat-trapping gases known to cause climate change. Imperfect as the bill was (it was opposed by Greenpeace and Friends of the Earth), it represented the first step toward measurable cuts in carbon dioxide emissions, which the country had stubbornly resisted for decades. Most notably, the bill included a cap-and-trade scheme that sets government limits on total emissions and allows polluting businesses to buy credits from cleaner operations. It had the support of large corporations and high-emission industries, because it leaves more flexibility than a straightforward carbon tax. Some say it's great for being gamed. "Cap and trade . . . is almost perfectly designed for the buying and selling of political support through the granting of valuable emissions permits to favor specific industries and even specific Congressional districts. That is precisely what is taking place now in the House Energy and Commerce Committee," wrote John Broder in the New York Times on May 17, 2009, in the weeks leading up to that historic congressional vote. If Europe's early experience is indicative, success for cap-and-trade will depend on oversight and management. Environmentalists warn that fossil-fuel industries negotiated free handouts of emission allowances as part of the political bargain, which does little to reduce the emission of greenhouse gases or the dependence on foreign oil or dirty coal.

However there is a positive precedent. The 1990 Acid Rain Program implemented a similar cap-and-trade system to reduce sulfur dioxide emissions. It limited the amount that can be emitted annually and put a tradable value on allowances. It was a market-based program that offered financial incentives to find the most cost-effective solution and helped reduce the sulfur emissions by a significant amount (ca. 50 percent) over the following years. It became part of the Clean Air Act, a piece of legislation that also regulates the emissions from boat engines.

Solving one problem by creating a new one

Clean air was on legislators' minds when they ushered in the age of methyl tertiary butyl ether (MTBE), a volatile, flammable and colorless liquid that doesn't mix with water. As an oxygenate fuel additive it was supposed to make gasoline burn cleaner and help reduce smog-forming compounds in automobile and boat exhausts. It was readily available and did not boost the price of gas by much, so it was adopted in California and several other states. It was a patch solution that tried to address the larger problem: Too many fossil-fuel burning vehicles in crowded places cause bad air, bad water, and bad health. But soon evidence mounted that MTBE might be a dangerous groundwater contaminant. The EPA's Office of Water concluded that available data support the conclusion that MTBE is a potential human carcinogen at high doses. So while trying to solve the smog problem, we created a groundwater problem. When MTBE was found in dangerous concentrations around marinas and boat launch ramps (i.e. on California's Lake Tahoe), stemming from fuel spills, unburned fuel, or underground storage tanks, the alarm bells went off. MTBE now is banned by many states and was replaced by ethanol, which also is an oxygenate, but one that's made from corn. Supposedly that's better for the environment, but not for boat engines, as we'll see later.

Diesel, on the other hand, is different, but is it necessarily better? Well, it depends on the technology that is used to burn it. As a kid I loved the whiff of sweet and heavy bunker oil when I was strolling the piers of the harbors in the Adriatic. The aroma invoked fantasies about far-away places that I wanted to visit one day. Later, I forgot about it and became infatuated with sailboats. But in the last few years it came back. Paddling and sailing on San Francisco Bay, often in close proximity to gargantuan container ships that steam in and out of it, and seeing the endless throngs of container-laden trucks clog the freeways, the sweet smell of cheap bunker oil no longer elicits dreams of exotic places, but concerns about respiratory health. Inhaling that stuff is akin to smoking a stogie, minus the buzz. If there's reason to be concerned about cigarette smoke— and not even tobacco companies can deny that anymore—there was as much reason to be alarmed about the position of my old house downwind from the Port of Oakland, and the cloud of sulfur and nitrogen oxide that was constantly wafting by.

But there is another reason for my diesel-phobia and it's linked to cruising. Down the coast of Croatia, up the coast of California, or helping with a delivery from New Jersey to Maine, I often ended up breathing nearly as much diesel exhaust as an attendant at a truck stop. That's only a slight exaggeration, but a sailboat trip where 80 percent or more of distance is covered under engine power, is hard to qualify as such. Maybe one should call that trawler sailing. It wasn't so much that the boats were junk or that the crews were too lazy to bend on a sail. The chief culprit was time constraint. Sail a ship to schedule, and you'll end up on the rocks or in the carbon column. If you have a boss, a family or some deadlines staring at you, and the wind is taking a siesta, reaching for the ignition key to fire up the "diesail," is standard operating procedure. So rule number one for sustainable sailing: Take more time to get where you want to go.

Cleaning up diesel

Air quality data of 2007 shows that about 144 million people in the U.S. live in areas that have unhealthy levels of smog. About 88 million people live in areas where they breathe too much particulate matter. Both pollutants contribute to health problems that include premature mortality, aggravation of respiratory and cardiovascular disease. Beyond the impact on air quality, diesel exhaust has been classified by the EPA as a likely carcinogen for humans. Children, people with heart and lung conditions, and the elderly are suffering the most. That means billions are spent to treat health issues caused by diesel exhaust. That's why legislation is curtailing tailpipe emissions of diesel engines in a progressive way, first on the road and the rail, then on the water. And California, bankrupt as the state might be, has been leading the way.

In 2008, the Los Angeles Times reported that the California Air Resources Board (CARB) proposed mandatory installation of so-called exhaust traps on 230,000 heavy-duty trucks and the replacement of 350,000 older, dirty engines between 2010 and 2025. At a cost of $5.5 billion that rule, which applies to trucks and buses, is the most expensive air pollution regulation in California's history. But doing nothing, again, would be far more costly, at least in the estimation of state officials who project that the measure could save nearly 10,000 lives in the first 15 years and save up to $68 billion in healthcare costs.

If trucks are bad, ships are much worse. And where they both appear in large numbers, the fallout from diesel pollution is the greatest. Having escaped regulation for the most part, ships have been allowed to spew toxic emissions from low-grade bunker oil that's high in sulfur and nitrogen oxide. The fuel in these ships averages 27,000 parts per million (ppm) of sulfur. By comparison, diesel trucks must use fuel with only 15 ppm. But that is changing now. Navigating in corridors along populated coasts, or sailing in and out of ports, cargo ships are now required to burn higher-grade diesel with reduced sulfur content. That's more expensive, but also cleaner. When they are out in the open ocean, these restrictions don't apply. Not yet, at least.

Under a plan that was proposed by the U.S. and Canada, ocean-going ships would have to burn higher-grade fuel that cuts sulfur levels in the fuel first to 10,000 ppm by 2010 and to 1,000 ppm by 2015, or install pollution-control equipment. A similar crackdown on nitrogen oxide levels is expected to begin in 2016.

In May 2004, the EPA finalized the Clean Air Nonroad Diesel Rule that took effect in 2007 and spelled out requirements for marine diesel fuel with 99 percent less sulfur content to reduce particulate matter. In 2008, the agency rolled out a tiered program aimed to curtail emissions from marine diesel engines below 30 liters per cylinder displacement, which include engines for recreational boats. The hope is to cut particulate matter and nitrogen oxide emissions by as much as 90 percent and 80 percent, respectively.

In the U.S., the brunt of regulatory measures affects manufacturers, not consumers. "Boat owners are in no way responsible for making modifications to their current engines to meet the standards or subject to any penalties as a result of this rule," is one of the key sentences in a EPA document about more stringent emission standards for small marine engines. But boaters are a tiny subset of the carbon society. "Pleasure boat engines are minute in numbers compared to [those] on the highway, and [boats] spend most of their time tied up in their slips," said Douglas Rose, a manager at engine manufacturer Volvo Penta. "So the return on investment from chasing boaters is nowhere near as great as cleaning up trucks."

Trying to understand where things with auxiliary diesel engines stand requires a solid understanding of government logic, if indeed there is such a thing.

In 2009, most marine pleasure engines were regulated by EPA Tier 2, Rose explained. But engines under 50 hp were subject to regulations for off-highway industrial engines, which were subject to Tier 3, meaning a more stringent set of rules. Larger engines use common-rail fuel systems and electronic injection control, but fall under Tier 2. Starting in 2012, Tier 3 requirements for marine engines with more than 50 hp will start to take effect, and depending on horsepower and displacement, they should be fully phased in by 2015. "What our strategy for these engines will be, is difficult to say at this time," Rose said. "For sure, it will include electronic injection control, and either common rail or unit injectors. It may require some sort of exhaust after treatment." Other technologies such as advanced combustion control and electronically controlled exhaust gas recirculation, that are already installed in industrial engines, might also surface in the marine market. Tier 4 which has two sub-tiers (A and B) will reach marine applications in 2014 and feature more fancy technology like selective catalyst reduction with urea injection or exhaust gas recirculation with diesel particulate filters, perhaps some combination of both. "These are the areas that are currently at the forefront of technology, so guessing which way the marine industry will go is a real crap shoot," Rose tried to keep his options open.

Common-rail technology that has brought a new level of fuel efficiency to diesel engines for cars and trucks is also available for boats, but for the time being only in marine engines above 100 hp. A high-pressure fuel rail supplies diesel to individual solenoid valves, which produces a more thorough combustion. It has transformed the European market for passenger cars for two reasons: In place where fuel is extremely expensive, cars with great gas mileage are in high demand. Second, turbocharged common-rail engines have become so quiet and powerful, they resemble gasoline engines. If you get a tax break *and* better mileage, choosing diesel was a no-brainer. Although this trend has changed somewhat as diesel now costs nearly the same as gasoline and taxation also increased, it explains the high percentage of diesel Volkswagens, BMWs, Fiats, Renaults, Volvos, etc. So if common-rail is the stroke of genius that produced clean and cultivated car engines, why is it so hard to find an engine under 100 hp that was explicitly designed for marine use? The reason, experts explained, is that the market for small diesel engines is not big enough and that the cost of the complex common-rail technology and its electronics is much easier absorbed by larger motors. Besides, there's no need for common-rail in small engines, because as things stand, they are able to meet current emission standards with indirect fuel injection. However, when Tier 4 requirements become applicable to marine engines, they too will become more sophisticated with particulate filters, catalysts etc. Alas, they will become more expensive, too. The saving grace is the sparse use of the average recreational boat, which helps extend its useful life far beyond that of a car (or a computer). The same holds true for a boat's diesel engine, which doesn't run a whole lot of hours if it is only used on weekends or for the snow bird cruise in spring and in fall. Sure, it requires maintenance as it ages, but with the proper care it will "run good" and clean. And that's probably as good as it gets for all the existing diesel engines that use older technology. "Bad performance equals high emissions and a larger carbon wake," said Greg Eck, special projects manager at Yanmar USA. "A 50-cent savings can turn out to be costly, if for instance you buy a third-party oil filter that fits but isn't rated for the higher pressure in our engines." Here are Eck's top tips:

- Do the maintenance: Stick with the recommendations of your engine manufacturer, perform the tune-ups on time and use genuine parts. If you visit places where original spares are hard to come by, stock up on air, oil and fuel filters.
- Keep it clean: Use clean fuel, change the filter and make sure the tank is clean, too. Once algae start growing, the filters, even new ones, tend to clog very quickly.
- Let it breathe: Sailboats can have cramped engine compartments that do not provide enough air flow, so the motor runs rich. It gets more fuel than it needs, it smokes more than it should, and it discharges unburned fuel into the water. To diagnose this problem, Eck suggests running at full throttle for five minutes, then opening the engine room hatch. If it is difficult to open because there is a pressure difference between outside and inside, or if rpm picks up when you open it, the engine doesn't get enough air.
- Break it in: You have to work a new diesel or it will fail. How an engine is operated during its first 50 hours of operation determines how long it will last and how well the engine will perform over its lifetime. Check the manufacturer's handbook and follow the instructions.
- Do not operate the engine at low idle or at low speed and light load for more than 30 minutes at a time. Since unburned fuel

and engine oil will adhere to the piston rings when operating at low speeds for long periods, this will interfere with proper movement of the rings and the lube oil consumption may increase. If operating engine at low speed and light load, you must race the engine to clean the carbon from the cylinders and fuel injection valve.

- When leaving, don't idle at the dock. "Get out into open water and run the engine at 90 percent of wide-open throttle, so the piston rings get seated," Eck recommended. Once cylinders become glazed, you'll burn oil. If the engine and the exhaust are cold and the engine runs rich, the mixture condenses on motor parts. Before shutting the engine off, let her idle for a few minutes until the engine gets to the lower end of the operating temperature.

- Biodiesel: Yes, you can, but be aware of the downsides and check with your engine manufacturer first. "It requires more maintenance, there is more water in the fuel, and sometimes less lubricity, which wears out fuel-injectors quicker and could shorten the useful life of the fuel system's components," Eck cautioned.

- Use the proper prop: If the engine is rated for a maximum rpm of 3000, it should reach it at wide-open throttle. If your boat reaches hull speed at 2500, don't go to a higher-pitched propeller, because that might well overload the engine. If you decide to change propeller, consult a professional.

- Be a good citizen: Keep up with maintenance to retain the manufacturer's warranty and satisfy owner/operator's obligations toward the EPA. It's all part of a sustainable sailor's conduct.

SOURCES:
Volvo: www.volvo.com/volvopenta
Yanmar Marine: www.yanmarmarine.com
Nonroad Diesel Rule: www.epa.gov/nonroad-diesel/2004fr/
    420f04029.htm

Gasoline engines

Just as diesels are becoming leaner and cleaner, gasoline in- and outboards are getting cleaned up too. That's important because, for the foreseeable future, the majority of boats will still come with combustion engines. The reason is simple: It takes much more power to move a boat through the water than a car down the road, and pound for pound, a gallon of gasoline or diesel still delivers the most energy for this purpose. Not until that equation changes substantially, will internal combustion engines disappear. Even diesel-electric and hybrid systems that are beginning to surface in pleasure boats, rely on combustion technology in the generators that produces electric power for the propulsion.

The development of cleaner marine engines has received impulses from the California Air Resources Board (CARB) that sets emission standards that often exceed those by the EPA. CARB was formed in 1967 to improve the state's air quality by regulating vehicle emissions, because a federal act allowed California to set its own emissions standards. And what happens in California tends to happen on the federal level, only with a few years delay. Sometimes this takes a while and a change of the political landscape. Take the federal fuel-efficiency mandate for vehicles of 35.5 miles per gallon that was announced on May 19, 2009 and was slated to take effect in 2012. This plan mirrors the one that was first proposed by California in 2002, but had been stalled by lawsuits and the oil-friendly Bush administration. This is worth remembering, because it influences what kind of boat engines can be sold in the U.S. Take, for example, CARB's star rating that was introduced for outboard engines to identify their efficiency. The one-star standard of 2001 became the EPA standard in 2006 and identifies outboards that produce ca. 75% fewer emissions than conventional carbureted two-stroke engines. However, most outboard manufacturers choose to certify engines to the more stringent CARB two-star and three-star levels, because they were well below the EPA standards and that earned them credits for the average emissions of all their models combined. The two-star label identifies engines that meet CARB's 2004 exhaust emission standards, which are 20 percent below the one-star levels. Another step is the three-star label that applies to engines that meet CARB's 2008 exhaust emission standards, which are 65 percent lower than those of one-star engines.

The CARB rules were devised in the wake of the EPA announcement of Emission Standards for New Gasoline Marine Engines in 1996, which spelled out a phase-in period for cleaner, more efficient and better performing engines. The Gasoline Marine Final Rule, which was published after a period of negotiations between the government and the marine industry, established emission standards for new spark-ignition outboards and gasoline engines in personal watercraft and jet boats. Inboards were not included in this rule. The goal was to control exhaust emissions and a reduction of hydrocarbon emissions by 75 percent by 2025. Some of the worst hydro-carbon polluters, it was determined, are non-road engines, i.e. the two-stroke motors found in outboards, jet skis, and lawn-care equipment. "Non-road sources as a whole on average contribute ten percent to average HC inventories," the EPA stated. "HC contributes to ground level ozone which is known to cause irritation to the respiratory system. Controlling emissions from these engines will help reduce adverse health and welfare impacts associated with ozone."

It set the stage for the proliferation of fuel-injected two-stroke and four-stroke engines that the EPA also said would "provide easier starting, faster acceleration, quicker throttle response, and a reduction in smoke, fumes and noise. Significant improvements in fuel economy could provide hundreds of dollars in fuel savings. Furthermore, the new fuel systems and engine designs will relieve boaters from the hassle of mixing fuel and oil." Not to forget, these new marine engines were covered by a three-year or 200-hour warranty, more than double the standard warranty offered by manufacturers at the time.

Since the EPA regulates emissions not technologies, engine manufacturers were given considerable flexibility to choose their own path, developing clean technology for the more upscale models, which earned them credits for their "corporate average emission standard." This allowed them to keep some older two-stroke models in the product line, provided the overall average did not exceed the EPA standard. The process was designed to phase in the new without being "overly burdensome or costly to manufacturers or consumers, while still achieving the overall pollution reduction goals of the program." An outboard manufacturer that has accrued a good corporate average emission standard could legally sell carbureted two-stroke engines until January 1, 2010, although cleaner, more efficient engines have been available for quite some time. The customer can buy them without having to worry about being penalized for his choice by the federal government. It is a system that puts consumer choice first, but is it necessarily the best for the environment?

In 1998, the California Assembly Bill 2439 (Bowen Bill) sought to ban two-stroke engines above 10 hp from recreational use on California lakes or reservoirs that serve as domestic water supplies or are connected to a drinking water supply distribution and treatment system. It was opposed by the recreational boat building industry and was defeated, but it pointed out the general issues of two-stroke outboards. Its text and an analysis were published on www.rbbi.com, a Web site owned by Polson Enterprises: "According to the author, emissions from two-stroke marine engines rank among California's largest sources of toxic water pollution. The high emissions are due to the inefficiency of the two-stroke engine, which requires fuel and oil to be mixed prior to use, causing incomplete combustion. A U.S. Environmental Protection Agency study shows that approximately 25 percent of the fuel/oil mixture from two-stroke engines is emitted, unburned, in the exhaust . . . U.S. EPA certification data demonstrate that two-stroke engines produce over eight times the hydrocarbon emissions produced by four-strokes, on average. Discharges to water by these motors include known carcinogens such as benzene and toluene. While approximately 10 to 15 percent more expensive, four-stroke engines on the market today are more efficient, contain internal oil systems not requiring premixing with (and thus discharge with) gasoline, and produce fewer air and water emissions."

I asked Martin Peters who handles communications for Yamaha, how two-strokes were doing in the market before the mandated sales stop. "As anyone in the industry can tell you, market share for two-strokes has been shrinking for many years," Peters explained. "Obviously, Yamaha was very early to market with a broad selection of four-strokes, and that has paid off in EPA credits. It has paid off for customers in many ways; the benefits of four-strokes are well known." But, he continued, Yamaha also recognizes that the market still demands two-strokes, mostly because of their favorable power-to-weight ratio and lower operating cost. "A good example of where two-strokes really shine is in the bass fishing arena. As you may know, speed and hole shot are important, which means weight is important. This is why two-strokes still dominate in that arena." Of course, Peters is right from the vendor's perspective, because his company has earned the right to continue to sell these engines. And a fisherman who wants maximum speed for minimum money has the right to buy and use a two-stroke engine as long as applicable laws are not violated. But from an eco-centric perspective, I don't know how discharging benzene and toluene into a closed body of fresh water and fishing in it, could qualify as sustainable practice. Governments in Europe banned the use of two-stroke outboards on freshwater lakes decades ago, for that exact reason. "The effort to reduce the weight of four-stroke outboards is ongoing," Peters said. "Hopefully, [these] changes will fill the need in the marketplace once only filled by two strokes." After all, the purchase price is only a small portion of the cost of an engine over its lifespan.

In September 2008, the EPA came back with more stringent exhaust emission standards for new spark-ignition in- and outboard marine engines, personal watercraft and generators and other non-road engines. The goal was to reduce the emissions of carbon monoxide, nitrogen oxide or hydrocarbons, which contribute to the formation of ozone. These standards were required by the Clean Air Act and included provisions for evaporative emission standards from fuel lines and tanks that have not been addressed before. They also were in line with the requirements that were adopted by CARB before. Like in 1996, the industry was given time to phase in the new technology and adopt new supplier schemes. The EPA also stated that modifications to exhaust emission requirements for high-performance inboard engines should reflect the "limitations of catalyst technology on these engines." With the new controls, the EPA estimated, volatile organic compound and CO pollutants from marine spark-ignition engines will be further reduced by 70 and 19 percent, respectively, by 2030. The control of evaporative emissions includes fuel tank and fuel line permeation, diurnal fuel tank vapor emissions (which happen when the tank cools overnight), and refueling emissions. So manufacturers are required to develop new fuel lines, both inside and outside the motor and tanks.

Starting with the 2010 model year, the emission standards for outboard and personal watercraft engines also are getting tighter and will have to be met with better fueling systems and in-cylinder controls, whereas the rules for sterndrive and inboard engines will require three-way catalysts, closed-loop fuel injection and failure diagnosis for the emission control system, similar to what's used in cars.

SOURCES:

Emission Standards for New Nonroad Spark-Ignition Engines, Equipment, and Vessels www.epa.gov/otaq/regs/nonroad/marinesi-equipld/420f08013.htm

Emission Standards for New Gasoline Marine Engines www.epa.gov/nonroad/marine/si/420f96012.htm

Choosing an outboard

Bringing the engines into compliance with EPA regulations is the manufacturer's job, but sailors still have to do some homework if they want to find an outboard that satisfies their requirements and goes easy on the environment. Weight, of course, is a big consideration besides horsepower, especially for small boats and tenders, because it influences performance and portability.

* **Two-strokes:** Simple and cheap they are, so they still have a following in a few places, but clean or efficient they aren't. One up-and down stroke of the piston produces one revolution of the crankshaft. The fuel-air mixture in the cylinder is compressed before it's ignited by the spark plug, which pushes the piston down. At the piston's lowest point, the intake and exhaust ports open simultaneously, a new charge of fuel and air rushes in, pushes out the exhaust gases, plus a considerable amount of unburned fuel and oil, which produces the blue smoke and the rainbow colors of the oil sheen in the water that used to be common around outboard-powered boats. The cleaner cousin of the carbureted two-stroke has a fuel injection and an electronic control unit that regulates the gas supply from the fuel pump. These engines are a step forward because the gasoline is better atomized for cleaner, more complete burn, more efficiency and more power. Pro: Powerful, light, good acceleration, simple maintenance, low purchase price. Con: High water and air pollution through unburned oil and fuel, poor fuel efficiency, loud, maintaining correct mixing ratio of fuel and lube oil to prevent motor from seizing, high wear and tear. Fuel-injected models do better on efficiency, burn less oil (it does not have

to be mixed manually with the fuel), and emit less hydrocarbon than the carbureted version.

- **Four-strokes:** They have intake and exhaust valves at each cylinder head, plus fuel injection systems. The intake valve opens during the downward stroke of the piston to release fuel into the combustion chamber, then closes. As the piston rises on the second stroke the fuel-air mixture ignites and forces the piston down for stroke number three. As it rises again for the fourth stroke, it pushes the exhaust gas through the exhaust valve that has opened and completes one revolution of the crankshaft. It's a cleaner process since intake and exhaust valves are not open at the same time. Fuel can't escape, unless it is completely burned and lubrication oil remains entirely separate in the crankcase. Pros: Cleaner, less polluting, more fuel efficient, quiet and smooth, no escape of unburned oil and fuel. Cons: More complex and expensive to maintain, bulkier than two-strokes, although light four strokes are available now.

To provide some sense of how two- and four-strokes compare in fuel economy, Nissan published a fuel-consumption chart that shows approximate numbers for their outboards. Comparing the numbers for engines of identical power, the difference is staggering, with four-strokes winning hands-down. At 5 hp the four-stroke sips 40 percent less gas, at 10 hp the difference was 27 percent and at 25 hp a four-stroke consumes a nearly one third less per hour. When comparing the weight of different models and makes, it's important to consider the number of cylinders. A four-stroke, one-cylinder Nissan 6-hp outboard suitable for sailboat propulsion weighs ca. 60 pounds, while Yamaha's 2-cylinder model of equal power is specified at ca. 80 pounds. A two-cylinder two-stroke 25 hp Yamaha weighs about 105 pounds, while a 3-cylinder Nissan four-stroke tips the scales at nearly 180 pounds. Finding the best outboard takes some legwork and the analysis of specifications, not just a glance at the price tag.

As outboards continue to get cleaner and lighter in incremental steps, they are also getting closer to the limits of combustion technology. Gas-powered outboards have not reached the end of their development," said Steve Fleming, communications director at

Mercury Marine. "Weight reduction is a continuous target, especially in the small-outboard category. Large outboards will likely see the development of catalyst technologies not unlike in the automotive world, except the requirements of outboard catalysts that operate in marine environments will require unique designs to combat corrosion, especially in salt water environments." Alternative fuel systems are largely being developed by the automotive world, Fleming continued, because of high resource requirements and the influence the auto industry will have on the availability of specific fuel types. "Until those parameters are established and accepted by the public, the marine market will have a hard time driving this development." Fleming acknowledged the increasing popularity of electric outboards, but thinks they have two strikes against them. "One of the benefits of small outboards is their portability. If a customer has to tote about an electric outboard and its required battery and cables, it becomes much less portable. Also, the ability to find places to recharge batteries, as well as the length of time required to charge them (compared to filling a fuel tank), is still an issue, just as it is with electric cars."

SOURCES:
Mercury Marine: www.mercurymarine.com
Nissan Outboards fuel table: www.nissanmarine.com/tech_talk/
    gas_mileage.html
Yamaha: www.yamaha-motor.com/outboard

6

The Fuss Over Fuels

Biodiesel

For quite some time now, biodiesel has been getting the attention of eco-minded car and boat operators. It is an improvement that goes back to the 1990s when the CARB mandated formulation changes for petroleum diesel fuel to reduce emissions of sulfur oxides, carbon monoxide and unburned particulate matter, also known as soot. CytoCulture, a biotech company in Richmond, California, said that blends of biodiesel with reformulated petrodiesel were "shown to improve the efficiency of combustion of the petroleum (in addition to diluting the noxious compounds) and thereby reduce emissions of sulfur oxides, carbon monoxide and particulates." The company also pointed out mechanical advantages of biodiesel's higher lubricity that protect against wear in the fuel and injector pumps. Because of its positive properties, biodiesel was marketed as an alternative fuel in some places (i.e. Europe), but only as additive (i.e. in California), because of state laws and manufacturer warranty concerns.

Unlike petrochemically refined diesel, biodiesel is manufactured from vegetable oils (e.g. soy, canola, sunflower seed) or animal fats, and involves the base-catalyzed transesterification of fatty acids with methanol. "It's imported from the Midwest, not from the Mideast," quipped Deedee Chatham, director of business development at Hudsonecofuel, a Rhode Island-based biodiesel marketing firm. There are few doubts that biodiesel gets the job done. By taking a 28-foot Zodiac 35,000 miles around the world in the early 1990s, the Sunrider expedition proved that it is a viable alternative fuel. EARTHRACE, the wave-piercing trimaran that set a record by circumnavigating the world in a little less than 61 days, ran on pure biodiesel.

Advocates point out the list of advantages: It's renewable, unlike fossil fuels. It's clean and produces fewer emissions in almost all categories compared with petrodiesel. It's good for the engine because it creates mechanical advantages through better lubricity. It doesn't smell or smoke. It's biodegradable so spills are a little less harmful. It's versatile, because it can be made from canola, soy or more than 300 other crops, but also from seaweed, algae, tallow and fish oil. Liposuction, too is a possible source, if you are so inclined. It creates domestic jobs. It's safer, because biodiesel is less toxic and has a higher flashpoint than regular diesel. It's smart politics, because local production keeps the dollars at home.

Most diesel cars, trucks and boat engines can use this type of fuel, which is typically sold as a blend that contains between 5 and 20 percent biodiesel. "We noticed no difference to regular diesel," said Matt Gineo, manager of Old Port Marine in Newport, Rhode Island. "The short-term benefits are cleaner-running engines and a nicer smell, which some customers compared to fries. In the long run, we'd expect engines to suffer less wear because of biodiesel's better lubrication." Gineo emphasized that no changes or modifications to the engines were required. His experience with the fuel has made him a believer—"as long as it is readily available and the price is right." If it's cheaper, cleaner, better and made in the U.S., why is biodiesel still an obscure concept to many boaters? "Supply hasn't caught up with the hype," Chatham said. "Marina owners and fuel dock operators are critical for the distribution and they will come around if consumers ask for it. The other issue is resistance to change and perhaps some fallout from the ethanol scare."

Biodiesel doesn't attack old fiberglass tanks the way ethanol-enriched gasoline does, but there are a few simple things to keep in mind when switching over. "Change fuel and air filters early and often; then keep up with a regular schedule," explained Peter Bethune, the skipper of EARTHRACE. "Fuel efficiency is down slightly, because 10 percent of biodiesel is oxygen, which causes a fuller combustion and increases apparent fuel consumption." Because pure biodiesel tends to solidify at low temperatures, he recommends the use of B20 blend or heated fuel lines when boating in colder climates. The biodiesel handbook published by CytoSource suggests U.S. engine manufacturers stand by their warranties as long as a fuel meets the American Society for Testing and Materials standards. B20 blends of U.S.-made biodiesel do. However, CytoSource recommends contacting the engine manufacturer to be absolutely certain the warranty won't be affected. Yanmar approves the use of biodiesel in a 5-percent blend and recommends purchasing it from authorized suppliers. The firm however warns about abnormal wear of injectors, reduced engine life and affects on warranty coverage should the fuel not meet the applicable specifications, which are defined for pure biodiesel (prior to blending) by ASTM D-6751 in the U.S.

Some points boat owners should consider before making the switch:

- Biodiesel fuels contain more methylesters, which can deteriorate certain metal, rubber and plastic components of the fuel system. Verify that your engine and fuel system parts are compatible with biodiesel.
- Free water in biodiesel can clog fuel filters and produce bacterial growth.
- The high viscosity at low temperatures can cause fuel delivery problems, such as injection pump seizure, and poor spray atomization by injection nozzles.
- Biodiesel can affect elastomers used in seals, which could cause fuel leakage and dilution of the engine oil.
- It is important to maintain a supply of clean and fresh fuel. Regular flushing of the fuel system and tanks might be necessary.

RESOURCES:
National Biodiesel Board: www.biodiesel.org
CytoCulture Environmental Biotechnology: www.cytoculture.com
Hudsonecofuel LLC: www.hudsonecofuel.com
EARTHRACE: www.earthrace.net
Yanmar USA: www.yanmar.com

Ethanol

Attempts to clean up the air with cleaner-burning fossil fuels will be with us until zero-emission technologies become significantly more affordable and convenient. It is a problem that affects sailors to a lesser degree than boaters who rely exclusively on internal combustion for their mobility. After the ill-fated attempts with MTBE as an oxygenate, ethanol became the chosen additive. It is an oxygenated hydrocarbon compound with high octane rating. Higher-octane levels in gas produce a cleaner burn, which reduces some emissions. Ethanol is highly refined grain alcohol, approximately 200 proof, that is produced from crops such as corn, sugar cane or wheat, which many critics consider a bad idea since it causes price increases on the most basic foods. New technology will allow ethanol to be made from cellulosic feedstocks i.e. corn stalks, grain straw, paper, pulp, wood chips, municipal waste, or switchgrass. If used as fuel, ethanol is denatured, by adding gasoline. E-85 (a blend that contains 15 percent ethanol) is intended for engines that are specially designed to accept high ethanol content in fuels, such as the flexible fuel vehicles made by some car companies. Most boat engines, manufacturers said, are not ready for this switch.

In the spring of 2009, BoatU.S. and the National Marine Manufacturers Association joined other industry organizations to rally support from their constituents to shoot down a petition by the ethanol lobby, which proposed to increase the ethanol content in fuel from 10 to 15 percent. "We support renewable energy," said BoatU.S. Vice President of Government Affairs, Margaret Podlich, in a press statement. "However, our recent experience with a nationwide roll-out of E10, or a 10-percent ethanol concentration, leads us to believe there has to be a lot more science and unbiased testing before we can universally accept E15."

What makes ethanol problematic for boats is its hygroscopic nature, attracting water and mixing with it better than with gasoline. It is a solvent that loosens rust and debris in fuel systems, which can lead to engine contamination or failure. It also can attack plasticizers and resins from some plastic materials (i.e. in old gas tanks) that might not be affected by gasoline alone. Loose debris will plug filters and can interfere with engine operation. In combination with water ethanol is corrosive to some metals. Lastly, it conducts electricity, which can promote galvanic corrosion.

Ethanol has approximately 30 percent less heating value per gallon than gasoline (76,000 BTU vs. 110,000 to 120,000), which means the engine is burning more gas. The more ethanol is mixed into the fuel, the more the gas mileage will decrease, which creates the paradox of cleaning up the air by burning more gasoline. According to some estimates, E85 fuels would produce approximately 30 percent less mileage than pure gasoline. Again, the attempt to reformulate gasoline to clean up the air looks like it's defeating the purpose. To be on the safe side, outboard manufacturers recommend using gasoline with the correct octane rating. Most outboards in operation today will be OK with an E-10 blend, but not E-15 or E-20. Mercury said that "fuels containing higher levels of ethanol [than E-10] are not considered acceptable for use, and the use of fuels containing ethanol higher than 10 percent can void the warranty." Owners are also encouraged to check the condition of fuel lines, seals and tanks, especially on older (i.e. pre-1990) models and take corrective and preventive action to avoid problems, i.e. replacing components that are not made from ethanol-compatible materials. Leakage, softening, hardening, swelling or corrosion are all telltale signs for possible ethanol trouble that needs to be addressed immediately. Two-stroke outboards should experience little or no decrease in performance with E-10 blends, as long as the tank is completely free of water prior to introduction of gasoline with ethanol. Otherwise, something known as "phase separation" could occur which might plug up the fuel filter and lead to engine problems. Phase separation could cause most of the ethanol and water to separate from the fuel and drop to the bottom of the tank. That leaves gasoline with much smaller ethanol content in the upper portion of the tank and mostly water and ethanol below. If the lower phase that contains most of the ethanol is all the engine gets, it spells trouble. Manufacturers also recommend replacement of old fiberglass tanks (pre 1991) because their resins were differently formulated and won't withstand exposure to ethanol. If in doubt, call the manufacturer. Old rubber components in a fuel system should be replaced with parts that are certifiably safe for use with ethanol. Under these provisions, spare filters are a must-have item for the on-board toolbox. Some manufacturers recommend the addition of filters to eliminate water from the fuel before it reaches the engine.

Some ethanol basics:

- Don't use fuel with ethanol content higher than 10 percent.
- Before switching to E-10 fuel, have the tank completely drained and cleaned to remove any accumulated water, built-up varnish and corrosion.
- Install a 10 micron fuel/water separating filter between the boat's fuel tank and the engine and change it every 25 hours of operation until there are no indications of excessive water and contaminants collecting in the filter.
- Buy name-brand fuel, if possible from the same station.
- Consider adding fuel stabilizer to fresh fuel to retard fuel aging.
- Maintain a full tank of fuel when the engine is not in use. This reduces condensation and the void above the fuel. It also minimizes the flow of air in and out of the tank that's caused by changes in temperature.
- When preparing to store a boat for extended periods, remove all fuel from the tank or maintain a full tank of fuel with a fuel stabilizer added.

Despite the drawbacks and a share of less than 10 percent in the U.S. market of liquid fuels (in 2009), ethanol is here to stay. It is likely to grow in importance because of federal mandates, which increase the share of ethanol in gasoline blends. Big oil companies are beginning to cooperate with farmers who grow typical ethanol crops like corn, sugar cane, grass etc. British Petroleum was getting ready to finance a new $250-million plant in Florida to produce better biofuels, the first that's built with money and know-how from Big Oil. BP and DuPont, another big industrial company, reportedly have been cooperating on the production of biobutanol, an alcohol fuel that is compatible with existing pipelines and car engines. Whether or not it will become a factor for boat engines remains to be seen, but the trend toward cleaner fuels for combustion engines will continue on many fronts. On the other hand it's also complicating matters since biobutanol or any other "wonderfuel" does come with its own set of issues, just like MTBE and ethanol did.

RESOURCES:
BoatU.S. Seaworthy Magazine www.boatus.com/seaworthy/
    ethanol.asp
Ethanol Plant Clean Air Act Enforcement Initiative www.epa.gov/
    compliance/resources/cases/civil/caa/ethanol/
DuPont: www2.dupont.com/Renewably_Sourced_Materials/
    en_US/biobutanol.html
Mercury: www.mercurymarine.com
Yamaha: www.yamaha-motor.com

Using less but going farther

While politicians and manufacturers are batting around the permissible percentage of alternative fuels for combustion engines to clean up the air, reducing fuel consumption and CO_2 emissions is well within reach of every boat operator. Whenever gasoline prices skyrocket, the demand diminishes, but if gas is cheap, few people care. Hopefully this will change, since burning one gallon of gasoline or diesel impacts the environment just the same, regardless of what's being paid at the pump. There are several things sailors can do to reduce their consumption of fossil fuels not just on the boat, but also ashore.

Following is a mixture of suggestions, ideas and alternatives. Some of them are pretty self-explanatory while others a little bit more arcane.

- Keep up maintenance: A well-tuned engine is more efficient. Only clean injectors spray the right amount of fuel into the combustion chamber. Fuel, oil and air filters should be on your list of regular maintenance chores. Water or dirt contaminates fuel filters and can lead to fuel starvation and an overloaded engine. Clean air filters are especially important for diesel engines.
- Avoid the idle: Even when you are parked for just a few minutes, e.g. while waiting in line at the fuel dock, shut her down. It's clean and saves gas.
- Keep your bottom clean: Slick is fast. Boats that are kept in the water stand to gain a lot by periodical bottom cleaning and maintaining a smooth, consistent coat of paint below the waterline.

- Check the prop: Damaged or wrong props can be very costly. Using the right prop for your application is a good way to boost the engine's efficiency.
- Store the dinghy: Sailboats often putter along with a dinghy in tow, which produces lots of drag, so the engine has to work harder and burn more gas. The 10 minutes it may take to hoist the inflatable on deck and stow it for a passage will boost your boat's performance and drastically reduce the fuel bill. Also fold away awnings, biminis and dodgers when they are not needed.
- Don't floor it: Get your boat into the groove to coax more miles from each gallon. When in doubt, consult the manuals or talk to the boat and engine manufacturers.
- Go light: Don't top off fuel or water, unless you plan a longer passage. Liquids are heavy: 50 gallons of water equal 400 pounds, that's weight you shouldn't be pushing around unless you absolutely have to. Take stuff off the boat after your trips.
- Go smart: Plan your trips with the most economical routing and use tide and current charts. A favorable push means less throttle, less gas, and less CO_2.
- Use instrumental smarts: Keep an eye on the fuel-flow meter (if you have one) and go for maximum efficiency, not maximum speed. Fuel-flow meters can help operators develop practices to increase the miles per gallon.
- Vary the pitch: Depending on load and operating altitude (air at higher altitude contains less oxygen, which reduces engine power), a change in propeller pitch can improve fuel economy and performance. Less pitch is more rpm and vice versa.
- Fold the prop: Folding propellers provide better performance because they create less drag when not in use. Under power these engineering marvels surprise with efficiency. Some models can vary the pitch while underway, corresponding to engine load.
- Add additives: Treated fuel can also have a positive impact, because it contains additives that disperse water, remove carbon deposits, and improve combustion. Not all additives work equally well, so consult your engine manufacturer before spending money. It also depends on the quality of the fuel that is available, which is a concern for long-distance

cruisers. Diesel additives can help remove carbon deposits and keep injectors clean, which is a prerequisite for efficient operation.

◆ Trim right: Sailboats have a boot stripe that helps gauge the trim when loading the boat with supplies. As they say: "She likes to float on her lines."

◆ Go ahead, re-power: New four-stroke outboards are up to 25 percent more fuel-efficient and new inboard diesels are getting really smart. Replacing an old smoke-spewing engine has several benefits because a modern power plant runs cleaner, burns less fuel, produces less exhaust and is more reliable.

◆ Cut back on the AC: On warm nights wind funnels can direct the air into the cabin through open hatches. Inside air circulation can be helped along by strategically positioned cabin fans. Install bug nets!

◆ Have a party: Invite family and friends to go "boatpooling." More people on one boat means fewer per-capita emissions and most likely more fun for the kids.

◆ Blow it up: If you trailer your boat, make sure the rig has properly inflated tires.

◆ Go by night: For long road trips in the middle of summer, consider driving at night when it's cooler, which reduces AC use, fuel consumption and carbon emissions.

◆ Turn it off: Using less electricity at home while you're gone sailing helps cut CO_2 emissions from dirty coal-fired power plants. Turn off the thermostat and restart it with a timer prior to your return. Use power strips with surge protectors that can be turned off to throttle the flow of so-called "vampire currents" to appliances and electronics while nobody uses them.

◆ Pack lunch: It saves money and gas, because it eliminates trips to the supermarket or restaurant.

◆ Sail more. It's about the experience, not about how far or how fast.

Fuel and oil spills

So far we have talked about the effects of burning fossil fuels, but they can pollute when they are spilled at the fuel dock. Many millions of marine engines are in use in the U.S. alone, and all of them need gas or diesel at some point. Gassing up a boat on the water is different from refueling your car and spilling fuel into water is a bigger headache than on land.

Diesel and gasoline are refined from crude oil. They contain metals and hydrocarbon compounds, which are thought to be toxic to larvae of fish, shellfish, and other marine organisms. The typical giveaway for a fuel or oil spill is a rainbow-colored sheen in the water, which can be removed. However that isn't enough to eliminate the effects since hydrocarbons can remain in the water column or accumulate in the sediment on the seafloor. Evaporation of fuel also plays a big role as it pollutes the air and adds to the smog, which hangs in the air visibly, especially on still, hot days when ozone forms easily. That's why the EPA has begun to regulate evaporative emissions from fuel tanks and lines.

When the oil tanker Exxon Valdez scraped a reef in the Prince Williams Sound in Alaska in 1989, more than 38,000 metric tons spilled into the ocean, fouling 1,300 miles of coast line, wrecking nature, fisheries, and people. After the initial shock had worn off, years of cleanup, finger pointing and litigation followed and many billions of dollars had to be paid out to mitigate the environmental and social damage. But the scars linger and the images of oil-crusted sea creatures haven't been forgotten. It was the mother of all oil spills, but it was not the last of them.

National Geographic reported that a total of 439 significant man-made oil spills were brought to the authorities' attention between 1989 and 2007, noting that the number of large spills (700 metric tons or more) has declined since the 1980s. Still, scientists of the National Research Council estimate that more than one million metric tons of oil enters the oceans each year, with spills from tankers and barges contributing only approximately eight percent. More than 46 percent are believed to be seeping from deposits in the ocean floor. The Joint Group of Experts on the Scientific Aspects of Marine Environmental Protection (GESAMP) in the UK estimates that 2.35 million tons of oil per year enters the global marine environment. About 15 percent is attributed to natural seepage while the rest is believed to emanate from oil storage facilities, refineries, tanker ballast water, spillages from commercial shipping and urban run-off. How much of it comes from pleasure boats? A 1998 U.S. study by LT Johnson estimates that on a national scale, recreational boating contributed less than one percent of the total volume of oil spills that are reported to the U.S. Coast Guard. Causes of such spills (mostly diesel, but also lube oils) could be sunk or abandoned vessels, careless fueling and bilge pumping.

Effective prevention starts with education on maintenance and fueling procedures, bilge and waste oil management, and tweaking the fuel-supply system. Of the types of oil spilled, diesel was the most common, followed by lubricating oil and then waste oil. The 1998 Boating Clean and Green Survey that was conducted for California Coastal Commission by San Francisco State University found that California boat owners think that these leaks occurred mostly during bilge pumping, followed by engine leaks and spills that occur when fuel is transferred.

Why fret about a scant one-percent problem? First, because it can be eliminated with proper technique and technology and second, one percent of a lot is still quite a bit. The California Coastal Commission estimated that one quart of engine oil spilled into one million quarts of seawater is concentrated enough to kill half of the exposed crab larvae. Other species like phytoplankton, fish eggs, and shellfish larvae can experience reproductive problems, according to Save Our Shores. Their DockWalker brochure claims that one pint of oil contaminates two acres of ocean, while the Monterey County Health Department said one gallon of oil is enough to contaminate one million gallons of seawater. In other words, very little oil or fuel has a big and measurable negative impact on sea creatures, because it degrades their habitat and health. But it doesn't stop there. Small organisms are part of the food chain, which means that they pass toxins in their bodies to their predators, which is a game that continues all the way up the food chain until poisoned fish or mussels end up on our dinner table.

Exacerbating the problem is the location where the spill is most likely to occur: Small-craft harbors that often don't have a good water exchange. They often resemble a bathtub, where water sits and warms and gets stirred by propellers and bow thrusters, which mixes spilled oil and fuel into the water column. Storm run-off from adjacent roads, gas stations or boat yards can add to the pollution, which also can cause sediment contamination.

Here are some suggestions to consider next time the boat needs gas: Fuel tanks on boats are much larger than in cars, so pumps at fuel docks tend to pump a higher volume than those at automotive filling stations. Boat fuel systems have an over-board vent through which fuel can spill into the water. Cars, on the other hand, use systems with a pump in the fuel tank to deliver the gasoline directly to the injectors at high pressure. This is good for fuel economy and performance and the environment since closed and pressurized systems do not let gas or air escape from the tank. Pressurized fuel systems for boats were outlawed in the U.S. in 1971, because of the dangerous possibility of gasoline collecting in the bilge in case of a leak, a recipe for fireworks if a spark would enter the equation. Hence the vent that lets air move in and out of the tank during fueling and while under way and in warm temperatures when the pressure inside the tank increases. When filling up an empty tank, the fuel displaces the air. If the fuel is pumped in faster than air can escape, the ensuing "burp" lets gasoline gurgle up and spill out through the vent. Another reason for inadvertent fuel spills is the temperature difference of fuel that is pumped from a cool storage tank into the tank of a boat that had been sitting out in the sun. "Resist topping off," BoatU.S. recommends, "and leave 10 percent of tank capacity empty to allow for fuel expansion."

If the vent can't handle the amount of escaping air, a more violent spillage can occur through backsplashing from the filling port on deck, so make sure the vent is not blocked. You also might want to ask the attendant to slow down the pump speed. (Good luck with that on a busy summer weekend when lines tend to be long and tempers short.) In any case, an absorbent collar and a spill pad spread out on deck can be effective remedies to minimize the effects of a burp or backsplash. Another good idea is to keep the boat floating level when refueling, or park the trailer on a level surface if you do it on land. A low-tech remedy to prevent overflow spills is to listen carefully for a change in the noise that is created by the fuel rushing down the supply line from the filling port to the tank. If the pitch increases, stop, because you are nearing capacity.

Being cautious is a good thing for clean refueling practices. Sometimes though, caution is not enough. Automatic nozzle shutoffs for instance should be the subject of healthy distrust. This might sound ridiculous, because they work just fine at the gas station. Alas, boats aren't cars, even though the principle of the shutoff is the same: Fuel flows through the pump's nozzle, passing through a small tube (called venturi) that operates on suction and creates a vacuum. It signals the nozzle to click off before an overflow can occur. As fuel flows through the venturi, air gets sucked through a sensing hole at the tip of the nozzle and up through the tube in circular fashion. It's fuel out, air in. Air gets mixed into the fuel that is being pumped into the tank. As the tank fills up, fuel rushes up the fill pipe, until it reaches the sensing hole in the nozzle. Now the circular pattern of air sucks in fuel through the sensing hole, which disrupts the airflow and triggers the automatic shutoff. Because fuel tends to get pumped faster at fuel docks, it rushes up the fill pipe faster than the automatic shutoff can react. If that happens, it shoots out the fuel port and soils deck, dock, and environment. The only remedy is keeping a close watch and a finely tuned ear on the fill port as long as fuel is being dispensed.

Trusting the fuel gauge can be risky too. Actually, the gauge is not to be blamed as often as the sending unit that's floating around in the tank and transmits an electronic impulse to the gauge to indicate the amount of fuel left. The reasons, BoatU.S. explained, could be compatibility problems between different manufacturers of gauge and sending unit, a sending unit that doesn't fit the shape of the tank, or damage to the sending unit. Other issues can concern calibration, float arm alignment, or electric problems. Boat owners are encouraged to inspect sending units visually to make sure they are not obstructed. Sometimes it might be necessary to check the wiring, grounding and the voltage of the sending unit. Lastly, a crude calibration by adding known quantities of fuel to the tank and checking the gauge readings can help too. If the readings are off, add hash marks with permanent marker to the gauge.

Effective spill prevention starts with sound judgment before the tank lid is unscrewed. Clean fueling is not just considerate practice, it's also required by federal law, which prohibits discharging oil or other hazardous substances into the water. Any amount that creates an oil sheen, even a few drops, should be reported to the U.S. Coast Guard National Response Center at (800) 424-8802. It's also illegal to treat a sheen by putting anything on it that will disperse, emulsify or coagulate it (i.e. detergents). At penalties of up to $32,500 failing to do so can become painfully expensive. If the venue is outside of the Coast Guard's jurisdiction, boaters are subject to prosecution under applicable state laws. The Green

Blue in the UK and the BoatU.S. Foundation (Help Stop the Drops) have published excellent information materials that help boat owners and marina operators prevent fuel spills or effectively respond to spillage. Save Our Shores started DockWalker, a grass-roots program that sends out volunteers to educate boaters about the importance of oil-spill prevention and handed out 400 clean-boating kits to recreational boaters in Monterey Bay, right next door to the National Marine Sanctuary.

Here are some useful suggestions for proper fueling and oil change procedures:

- Use a funnel, safety fill nozzle or a spill-proof canister when pouring fuel or oil.
- Always use an absorbent pad or collar.
- Do not rely on the hands-free or automatic shut-off features to alert you when the tank is full.
- Check fuel vent for obstructions.
- Fuel slowly and listen carefully for changes in pitch indicating that you are nearing capacity.
- Avoid topping off or overfilling to reduce the risk of fuel overflowing from vents. Keep in mind that fuel can shoot out through the fuel port after the pump is turned off.
- Check the fuel gauge for accuracy.
- Add a fuel/air separator in your tank's vent hose. It prevents fuel from pouring out the vent when vapor builds up.
- Keep up on fuel line maintenance to avoid slow leaks.
- If you suspect a spilling problem is a result of a faulty nozzle, report it to the dock attendant.
- When refueling from a jerry jug, use a funnel or a spout with an automatic stop device to prevent overfilling the gas tank.
- Close the vent on portable gas tanks when the engine is not in use or when the tank is stored.
- Store the spare fuel canister in a cool, dry place.

Oil change

- Keep an oil-absorbent sock or pad in your bilge to clean up oily bilge water.
- Install a bilge water filter.

- Before pumping the bilge, check water for oil sheens.
- When changing engine oil, disable automatic bilge pumps to prevent accidental overboard discharge of spilled oil. (Remember to reconnect the pumps later!)
- Don't drain oil into the bilge. Use drip pans and absorbent pads in the engine compartment.
- In small engine compartments, use a small pump to pull used oil from the fill port.
- Recycle used oil through your marina, a used-oil recycling center, or an automobile oil change business. Be careful not to mix used oil with any other liquids, because it'll make it harder to recycle and the mixture may be considered hazardous waste.
- Keep track of oil changes in a log to accurately determine when you need to replace oil.
- Transfer used oil or waste fuel in sealed containers and dispose of waste oil and contaminated items in appropriate oil/hazardous waste facilities. If your marina participates in the Clean Marina Program, it should provide these containers. If it doesn't, it's time to talk to management or find a place that follows best practices.
- Never use detergents to deal with spills—they might hide the sheen but add more toxics to the water. Instead, alert the marina or the Coast Guard.

Preventive care

- Keeping the engine tuned and checking carburetors and spark plugs can reduce the amount of unburned fuel and oil that escape with the exhaust gases.
- Examine seals, gaskets, and fuel lines to prevent leaks of oil and fuel from dripping into the bilge.
- Keep diesel injectors clean by regularly changing filters and using fresh fuel.
- Clean air filters ensure cleaner combustion.
- Change fuel filters regularly. Any contaminant in marine fuel can make your engine run dirtier, and less efficiently.

Useful accessories to keep the messy job of fueling and changing engine and transmission include disposable refueling mats and collars that protect the boat from hose and nozzle damage during refueling while catching and containing spills. A little bit more hi-tech are dedicated bilge filters that automatically remove oil, gas, diesel fuel and other hydrocarbon pollutants from bilge water before it is discharged overboard.

CARB and EPA requirements for portable fuel containers have brought about clever products that help prevent clumsy fuel spills with better spout design, variable flow, automatic venting and locking, airtight seal and child-safety features. Running a clean engine starts with clean fuel, so there is merit in considering the use of a funnel that simultaneously filters gunk and water from the gas or diesel before it enters the tank and the engine. These filtering funnels do not replace finer in-line fuel filters, but they can do some of the heavy lifting upfront.

SOURCES (education):
BoatU.S.: www.boatus.com/foundation/cleanwater/drops/
    products.asp
www.boatus.com/foundation/cleanwater/drops/Preventive.asp
The Green Blue: www.thegreenblue.org.uk/publications/
    documents/OilSpills.pdf

Photo 6.1 Clean engines need clean fuel. One of the most basic accessories is a fuel funnel with built-in filter. It's simple, cheap and effective, especially in remote locations where clean fuel is impossible to come by. *Parker Hannifin Corp.*

SOURCES (manufacturers):
Blitz fuel cans: www.blitzusa.com
Centek Industries bilge filter:www.centekindustries.com
Chadd Padd absorbent pads: www.chaddpadd.com
Racor filter funnels: www.racorcustomers.com

Calculating the carbon footprint

People want to know how much greenhouse gas they blow into the atmosphere. It has become a kind of obsession. The heating bill, the car commute, a plane ride, the electricity for gadgets and appliances, the food we eat, or a weekend sailing trip, everything is part of the carbon footprint. The gas that figures most prominently in those calculations is carbon dioxide (CO_2) because it was identified as a key contributor to global warming.

There are several reasons for calculating the personal carbon footprint, besides curiosity. Putting a number on consumption might help distinguish good from poor choices and result in a change of behavior. Planting trees or buying carbon offsets that help fund measures to combat climate change are other options.

But above all, this exercise might best be undertaken with fellow boaters who have similar concerns and see the point in saving the world while having fun. Dock mates can get together in friendly competition and out-green each other as they reduce the environmental impact of their boating activities. The winner gets a pair of Birkenstocks and a pound of hemp granola, or a case of naturally cloudy organic ale, bottle-fermented and brewed with solar power.

Scientific estimates put the average annual per-capita CO_2 emission in the US at approximately 20 tons. Burning a gallon of gasoline, as the EPA says, contributes approximately 19.4 pounds, a gallon of diesel ca. 22.2 pounds of carbon to the atmosphere. If a boat burns five gallons of gasoline per hour and the engine is run 100 hours per year, that's more than four tons of CO_2 for the planet. Ditto with the car that is being driven to tow the boat or haul the gear to the marina. Ditto with the genset, the running lights, the iPods, the radar, the chart plotter, the radio, the TV, the stereo etc. It all adds up.

In an article published by Professional Boat Builder magazine, Russell Bowler, vice president at Farr Yacht Design in Annapolis,

Maryland, estimates that it would take 31 trees to offset the emissions that are added to the atmosphere by burning 1,000 gallons of
diesel. "So a big boat that burns 100,000 gallons a year, produces
1,000 tons of CO_2. To sequester the carbon released from burning
fuel alone, 3,100 trees per year or 30 acres of forest need to be
planted." He then goes on to extrapolate the numbers for 5,000
mega yachts that are in operation at this time and concludes that
150,000 acres of forest must be planted annually to offset their fuel
emissions.

The Polson Enterprises' Web site BoatCarbonFootprint.com
calculates the more modest carbon footprint of small pleasure boats.
It is mostly focusing on powerboats, but some of the information
presented there can help with the calculation of a sailor's carbon
footprint, too. The first step is determining the number of gallons
of fuel you burn either by keeping a record in the logbook or by collecting the gas bills, much like you'd be doing for tax purposes if you
use your vehicle for business trips. Then multiply the number of gallons by the carbon factor of diesel (22.2) or gasoline (19.4) to calculate the tons of carbon emissions that come from the propulsion
systems of your boat. Or you can estimate the amount of fuel you
typically burn on one outing and multiply that by the average
number of outings per year.

Boatcarbonfootprint.com has some data from a 2002 survey regarding the mean number of boating days per year by vessel type, however without sample data for sailboats. An inflatable for instance,
which many sailors use as a dinghy, is shown to be in service for
13.62 days per year. Other ways to calculate engine gas consumption are the fuel consumption tables provided by the manufacturers
for any given engine (this might be difficult to come by for older
two-stroke outboards), or by duty cycle, which should reflect a mix
of different operating speeds.

Once the amount of gasoline consumption is determined and
the corresponding CO_2 emissions are calculated, how can a boater
go about offsetting the impact? The easiest way is to use one of the
carbon-offset calculators that are beginning to show up on boating-
related Web sites. Boatbookings.com, a charter agency, for instance,
offers such a carbon offset calculator, so charter customers can calculate their environmental impact and buy offsets from JP Morgan

Climate Care. "It's hard to determine what happens with the money, so I wanted to go with a trusted and recommended outfit," said managing director Tom Virden. "Credits that are purchased pay for UN-approved projects that reduce carbon emissions worldwide by helping to install wind farms, restore rain forests, and reduce outdoor waste burning." There are countless versions of emissions calculators available, but most are for general uses i.e. household or travel. Some of them are offered as a script that can be embedded into personal Web sites.

While carbon offsets have become a staple in the game of mitigating environmental impact, there will always be some uncertainties about how much of the money really goes toward the intended purpose, when it will be spent and how much good it really can do. Real change, hard-core environmentalists argue, starts with personal choice and behavior.

SOURCES:
Boatbookings.com: www.boatbookings.com
Carbonify.com: www.carbonify.com/carbon-calculator.htm
EPA Emission Facts:www.epa.gov/OMS/climate/420f05001.htm
EPA Transportation & Climate: www.epa.gov/otaq/climate/
     index.htm
EPA Personal Emissions Calculator: http://www.epa.gov/
     climatechange/wycd/calculator/ind_calculator.html
Polson Enterprises: www.boatcarbonfootprint.com
Travel Matters: www.travelmatters.org

Alternative Propulsion

Some sort of mechanical propulsion is necessary for all but the smallest of sailboats, if for no other reason than getting in and out of the marina berth. Advances in technology produced viable propulsion systems that use electricity to varying degrees. But fossil fuels are still at an advantage as far as energy density of the fuel is concerned, which makes them ideal for mobile application and to generate electricity, either through the onboard engine's alternator or through a dedicated generator. Now what if propulsion and power generation could be covered with greater efficiency by one system, just as it has been the case for decades on large commercial and military vessels? Those diesel-electric installations use generators to keep the lights on, while simultaneously providing the power for an electric motor that moves the vessel along. It is an intriguing idea that has been tackled by visionaries, who tried to shrink the massive commercial diesel-electric systems to fit pleasure boats and make them perform as well as, if not better than, standard diesels.

Others are betting on pure electrical power and better batteries that can store enough energy to replace diesel or gasoline engines. In Europe, several vendors have developed electric boats with AC motors and advanced battery technology in runabouts that easily reach planning speeds. At the center are lithium-polymer batteries which are now beginning to replace lithium-ion power packs in laptop computers.

The problem for alternative propulsion is battery capacity and operating range, which brings us back to energy storage and the advantages of fuel cell systems that are beginning to show up in pleasure boats. These systems have moved from utopia to possibility, even though several challenges still need to be resolved. But that is the intriguing aspect: It's a race toward a greener future, but no clear-cut favorites have emerged as yet. Clean is only one requirement, while affordability, practicability and scalability are as important. The best technology might not even win. In fact it rarely does. The political bargaining, the allocation of subsidies and emission credits, etc., have as much to do with the outcome of this competition as the work on the drawing boards. One of today's nutty propulsion professors might one day become the Henry Ford of low- or zero-emission boat engines, but it will happen in the lee of the larger and more lucrative automotive market. This leaves the door open for small companies to step in and come up with innovative solutions that others can license.

Diesel-electric propulsion

"To get more miles per gallon, go easy on the throttle." Every 12-step program that promises simple measures to improve fuel efficiency will suggest that. However, it's a little different with diesel engines, where puttering actually will do the exact opposite: It will increase the relative amount of fuel the engine consumes for every horsepower it produces. This, of course, is an oversimplification of technical matters, but it is one of the reasons why different propulsion concepts like diesel-electric and hybrids are beginning to show up in pleasure boats: they promise better efficiency. Diesel-electric systems use a diesel engine that is connected to an electrical generator. The power from the generator drives an electric motor and turns the propeller shaft. On larger yachts, such a system may have multiple generators and multiple motors, which are all connected to an electrical bus that distributes the energy as needed. This technology has been in use for about a century on large ships, and also on train engines.

Pushing a cruising boat with a displacement hull through smooth water at less than hull speed doesn't require a lot of power from a normally-sized engine. But this does not save fuel; the specific fuel consumption rate stays high. Conventional diesel engines should operate at 50 percent or more of their maximum power to improve specific fuel consumption. In other words, putting the throttle forward in nasty conditions, slamming into head seas or an adverse current is more efficient than puttering along, at least relatively speaking. At full throttle an engine will burn more fuel, but proportionally less so than if it is run at very low loads, meaning significantly below the "sweet spot" where the engine produces the most power for the least quantity of fuel.

Diesel-electric propulsion systems work by decoupling the propeller from the diesel engine, which becomes a generator that produces electricity. The trick is to have the generator supply "just enough" energy to the electric motor, while satisfying all other power needs on board. If the generator has to provide juice not just for the propulsion, but also for the cappuccino maker, the freezer, the navigation computer and the microwave, the engine must operate under high load, which means that specific fuel consumption goes down. However, this load-and-efficiency game doesn't go on forever. If the boat runs at theoretical hull speed, waves and resistance increase. Going a little faster requires a lot more power and fuel. But still, diesel-electric promises efficiency gains, if the generator's engine is kept fully loaded most of the time.

Manufacturers of diesel-electric systems claim that these gains have the potential "to fundamentally change the way boats are built and used." However fuel consumption charts that compare identical boats with conventional diesel and diesel-electric systems, are hard to come by. Nigel Calder, a noted cruiser and technical lecturer, investigated some of the efficiency claims in a series of articles for *Professional Boatbuilder* magazine in 2007 and found that the state of the diesel-electric art at the time did not yield the benefits the manufacturers were promising, at least not in relatively small cruising boats. "To capture efficiencies in a diesel-electric system, you have to be able to run the generator at variable speeds, and to keep it fully loaded at whatever speed it is running," Calder stated in response to an e-mail that sought comment on that matter. "For various technical reasons, this has turned out to be extremely difficult to do, and in any case at lower loads the generator is still relatively inefficient." He pointed out that diesel-electric systems add complexity because they have three elements—generator, conversion electronics and electric motor—between the engine and the prop. A conventional diesel just has the transmission, which incurs losses of its own, e.g. from the friction in the gears. There are also electrical losses that are associated with wiring and cooling circuits in diesel-electric installations. Calder stated in his article that "even in well-designed diesel-electric systems this can amount to 15 percent losses compared to the five percent associated with transmissions in conventional diesels." If batteries are added as buffers, charging and discharging inefficiencies can add up to 25 percent, which would make a standard diesel look pretty good. "If the losses between generator engine and propeller in diesel-electric installations exceed the losses of the transmission in conventional diesel engines and if it is designed to produce boat performance equal to a standard diesel engine at wide open throttle, diesel-electric will be less efficient when the boat is run at or close to full speed," Calder wrote.

On a 46-foot cruising yacht with displacement hull the switch from standard diesel to diesel-electric would make sense for speeds that are significantly below 7 knots, Calder concluded, which might not suffice for most users' needs. He also anticipated that the window of opportunity for diesel-electric applications in pleasure craft was closing, because of the continual improvements of conventional diesel technology and refinements in common-rail diesels. But the technology continues to improve and will continue to evolve, i.e. with the use of variable-speed generators that have load-following capabilities, and with more sophisticated control systems that optimize performance. Beside fuel efficiency, there are plenty of inherently advantageous features of diesel-electric propulsion: Having one diesel engine for propulsion and power generation instead of one propulsion engine and a separate diesel generator (or two propulsion diesels and one extra generator on a cruising catamaran) means less weight, which helps sailing performance, less maintenance and fewer oil changes, which constitutes savings in materials and cost. Being able to install the generator away from the propulsion motor(s) can help optimize weight distribution on the boat, which is another plus for performance. Because electric motors are quiet and diesel generators can be sound encapsulated, boats with diesel-electric propulsion tend to be quieter than boats with conventional engines. Lastly, any electric motor provides instant propulsion power, which is good for an emergency and very helpful for maneuvering the boat in the harbor, because there is no idle and instant torque.

Bruce Nelson, who handles marine sales at Glacier Bay, a Union City, California based manufacturer of diesel electric systems, said his company was in talks with builders, who wanted to offer diesel-electric options for some of the larger models of cruising catamarans. "At this time, the price for a diesel-electric system is approximately equal to that of a conventional diesel installation," Nelson explained. "The savings a customer can expect are coming from the lower amount of maintenance that is required and from the reduced weight, which means better fuel economy." Glacier Bay equipped a 46-foot charter catamaran with a diesel-electric system that replaced the two conventional 39-hp diesel engines and one electric generator. The boat first was in charter service in the Caribbean and now is stationed in Berkeley, California, where it also has undergone some system upgrades. Instead of oil changes every 150 hours for two conventional diesels, the generator requires only one oil change every 500 hours, Nelson said. That's a lot less oil and a lot more time between routine maintenance, which, all other things being equal, would be a reason for charter companies to consider diesel-electric. He also pointed out that diesel-electric does not require battery banks, which are heavy and subject to considerable inefficiencies during charging and discharging. "The benefit we hear most often about is the reduced noise on board," Nelson said. "The owners tell us that a quiet boat is a more social boat." Who could argue with that?

Serial hybrids

Like diesel-electric systems, serial hybrids have uncoupled the diesel from the propeller, but they also have a large battery bank to store electricity, which can be used for propulsion or for operating electrical appliances, without having to run a diesel generator. But traditional (i.e. lead-acid) batteries are heavy and don't provide the range that most cruisers are demanding from an auxiliary propulsion system.

Batteries are charged either at the dock by plugging into a shore power connector, by the alternator of the engine or by a diesel generator when under way. But contrary to diesel-electric systems, hybrids can use renewable energy from solar panels or a wind generator, which reduces the carbon footprint and provides insulation against rising fuel prices.

Calder calculated that it takes 8 kW of power and approximately two thirds of a gallon of diesel to motor along at 6 knots for an hour on his 46-foot cruising boat. If diesel costs $4 per gallon, the fuel cost of one hour under engine is $ 2.63. If the battery bank is charged from shore with the same amount of energy, plus 25 percent to account for the efficiency loss, the charge needs to be 10 kW. Assuming a price of 15c per kilowatt, that's $1.50 or 30 percent less than the cost of diesel. If diesel becomes more expensive the equation favors a hybrid even more, just as it does if a considerable part of the electric energy for the batteries are generated by the sun and/or wind.

A hybrid also can extract more power from the generator than required by the propulsion needs and store it in the battery bank. This process is known as buffering. When the batteries are fully charged, the engine is turned off and the boat runs only on batteries. When the charge decreases and reaches a certain point, the generator turns on automatically, which means the engine cycles on/off. When it is on and has to charge a run-down battery bank, it will operate under high load, which is what the diesel needs to be efficient.

Regeneration

When sailing along with the engines off, the propellers disengaged and spinning freely, a hybrid system can generate electricity. It's a principle that compares to towing generators that have been used for eons to convert kinetic energy into electricity. But the integration with the electric propulsion motor is quite slick, because it reverses the flow of power from the props to the battery and does not require towing an apparatus behind the boat on a long cable. "When hybrid propulsion is done right, it will make the boat go faster," Corsair's Dave Renouf surmised. "I call it electric sailing, which is actually a kind of motor sailing that uses the apparent wind. The e-motor runs off the batteries and pushes the boat along a little faster than it would sail, so it reaches hull speed. When it starts surfing, the props actually don't push the boat, but charge the battery." It works best on low-drag boats, such as catamarans or light-displacement sleds that go fast enough to bring the breeze forward and have an efficient rig to harness it.

It is also known as regenerative sailing and hybrid proponents think that overall boat speed could increase by up to a knot on average without net energy usage.

Regeneration, albeit in a different form, is an integral part of the hybrid car concept. Unlike traditional brake pads that clamp down on rotors to capture kinetic energy, which then dissipates as heat, regenerative braking systems use electric motors that "reverse the flow of power" to slow the car. This process generates electrical energy that charges the battery.

One of the pioneers of this concept is David Tether, formerly of Solomon Technologies and now heading Electric Marine Propulsion. Tether is working with Lagoon Catamarans on a hybrid version of the Lagoon 500 cruising cat and keeps installing his systems on a custom basis. "[Hybrid systems] remain the most powerful, most efficient and most capable systems in the world," Tether wrote from Trinidad, where he was busy launching a 55-foot catamaran with hybrid propulsion. "Yes, they are expensive and will continue to be somewhat expensive until the quantities are there. This is the reason why you typically seem them on higher-end yachts, but in the scheme of things they are worth every penny. How can you put a price on silence, or being able to go 29 days [while] regenerating and never burning a drop of fossil fuel, yet still having plenty of electricity for hot water, water makers, instruments, lights and auto pilot. For a catamaran, how can you put a price on having one oil change, one impeller, one oil filter and one muffler where there would have been three. For mono hulls, how can you put a price on now being able to have a generator, and only having one oil change instead of two?"

The obvious caveat is the use of fixed-blade propellers, which create considerable drag under sail, thus crimping the sailing capabilities especially in light air. But this issue could be addressed with feathering propellers that constitute a compromise between efficiency under engine power and reduced drag. Tether was also one of the first to incorporate power generation from renewable energy into his hybrid systems. On one of his early boats, he installed 15 solar panels, three of them for charging the house batteries and the other 12 wired in series for the propulsion system.

The key is balancing battery capacity and charging capability with propulsion demands between recharges.

Most hybrids don't have adequate battery capacity to go far under electric power without some sort of reliable generation. It's about a compromise between battery size, weight sensitivity and cost.

But the hybrid concept will benefit from lighter and more powerful batteries that are beginning to emerge in marine applications.

How well a hybrid works depends on the application. Boats that sail long distances with steady breeze can take advantage of regenerative capabilities, provided the system is well designed. House loads that draw on the batteries while sailing could be covered through regeneration, so running the generator wouldn't be necessary. However, that is not how most recreational sailboats are used. The more a boat is run under power, the less a hybrid system seems to make sense, because most likely you'd be using more electricity than renewable energy sources can produce, so you'd end up running the diesel generator.

Perhaps the most experience with hybrid systems of any sailboat manufacturer can be expected from French catamaran manufacturer Lagoon who introduced the 42-foot Lagoon 420 in 2007 with a battery-powered hybrid system. The successor model, the Lagoon 421, also is offered with a conventional diesel option, but the company is steadfast in its commitment to hybrid technology. "It was a learning experience, but we are ahead of the curve now," said Lagoon's US representative, Nick Harvey. "Lagoon sold 60+ hybrid systems in three years, which is the largest number of any recreational boat manufacturer. So far the best feedback comes from long-distance cruisers who like the regenerative capacity to charge batteries. They generate power in silence with a small CO_2 footprint." Harvey maintained that development continues and compared owning a hybrid to owning a computer that needs upgrades from time to time. One of the early challenges was synchronizing the generator and the battery charging state, which was corrected, "by implanting a new microchip in the charge monitor," according to Harvey. Hybrid systems on charter boats have a mixed record, he said, because often times they end up in the hands of inexperienced sailors "who use the boat differently and have a hard time understanding the technology." The running joke is that depleting the batteries overnight with high house loads might require running the boat's huge generator in the morning just to make a pot of coffee, which would negate any potential efficiency gains. As both sailors and charter companies become more experienced with the ins and outs of hybrid systems and as batteries become better and lighter, this might change.

Photo 7.1 The Lagoon 421 represents the second generation of the French company's cruising catamarans with hybrid propulsion. *Nicolas Claris, Lagoon Catamarans*

Since purchase decisions consider a variety of factors, a comparative glance at the specifications should be included in this discussion. The Lagoon 421 in a three-cabin layout is available in a standard diesel and a hybrid configuration, so it is a good example to gauge the differences. The hybrid comes with a 21.5 kW generator and two 10-kW electric propulsion motors, while the conventional version has two 40-hp or 75-hp diesels and an 11-kW generator. The hybrid's price was approximately $25,000 to $36,000 higher (depending on equipment) and its displacement was 2,600 pounds heavier than that of the same model with standard diesel installation. Harvey cautioned that the specifications and prices were preliminary, but even so they confirm that the decision for a cruising boat with hybrid propulsion would have to include more than just the initial price tag and the displacement numbers.

Parallel hybrids

This hybrid concept pairs conventional propulsion for high output with an independent, smaller electric motor that takes over when diesel operation is becoming inefficient, just like a hybrid car switches from gasoline to electric mode in stop-and-go-traffic, or for down-speed maneuvering. A parallel hybrid retains the mechanical connection between the engine and propeller shaft, with an electric motor turning the drive shaft of the main engine. In this arrangement it is possible to power the propeller both from the combustion engine, the electrical motor, or both at the same time. If the system is called on to do nothing but generate electricity, it doubles as a generator and it also allows regeneration while sailing, just like a serial hybrid does. The advantages of a parallel hybrid lie in the combination of motor and generator functions, which saves weight and cost. Calder suggests that having conventional diesel propulsion for high speeds or high-load operation in adverse conditions (such as getting off a lee shore) allows the electric drive to be downsized for slow cruising. This would make the whole system more efficient than a serial hybrid, because a smaller generator is easier to keep loaded and running efficiently.

Other benefits are the redundancy of propulsion systems, fewer failure points and a longer useful life of its components. If the diesel goes down, there is the electric motor that can get you back to port or at least out of a pickle. If an electric component fails, the conventional diesel can take up the slack. A well-engineered parallel hybrid could be leaner and less complex and longer lived because the alternator of the main engine doesn't have to charge the batteries, which reduces wear and tear. And lastly, there is the possibility of retrofitting existing diesel engines with a compact hybrid system that would add these benefits at reasonable cost and acceptable weight.

In 2008, Steyr Motors, an Austrian industrial company that used to manufacture mono-block marine diesel engines for OMC, introduced a compact hybrid system that covers many aspects of the parallel concept, except for the regenerative function. This system consists of a standard diesel from 50 to 300 hp that has an in-line 7-kW (ca. 9 hp) electric drive bolted to the flywheel. It is a neat solution that was developed in cooperation with Frauscher, an Austrian boat builder who produces boutique runabouts with gasoline, diesel, hybrid and electric propulsion. It's also an example of engineering your way around government-imposed restrictions, because on Austrian freshwater lakes, the operation of powerboats with combustion engines is severely restricted. "This engine is multifunc-

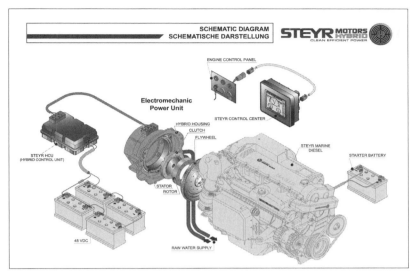

Photo 7.2 The schematic of Steyr's hybrid system shows that the electric drive is in line with the diesel engine, which makes it compact and suitable for use in small pleasure boats. *Steyr Motors*

tional," explained Stefan Frauscher, who handles sales and marketing. "It is a five-in-one deal: A conventional diesel for fast cruising, a generator to charge the batteries, an electric drive for silent, clean cruising or to dock and undock, a starter motor, and a booster for better acceleration, which requires the electric motor to automatically couple and decouple from the drive shaft."

According to Steyr, this hybrid is compact and light enough to be installed as a sailboat's auxiliary engine. In the U.S., the trawler company Island Pilot has installed a Steyr system in the DSe Hybrid, an unusual 40-foot cruising catamaran that also uses solar-electric power for propulsion and to cover the domestic energy needs. Sea Ray, the largest U.S. powerboat builder, said it was evaluating the hybrid concept for some of its smaller boat models.

Even though alternative propulsion systems still need fossil fuels to be practical, at least some of them can use renewable energy and regeneration to charge battery systems. Whether or not diesel-electric or a certain type of hybrid might revolutionize auxiliary propulsion remains to be seen. Maybe there won't be a clear-cut winner, as Glacier Bay's Bruce Nelson suggested. "There will be a market for both technologies," he said. Just what that market will look like and how big it's going to be, he wasn't quite ready to predict.

Pros:
- Quiet operation.
- Instant power and torque at all rpm, which is helpful in down-speed maneuvering.
- Better weight distribution, because electric motor and generators can be installed with more flexibility.
- Regenerative capabilities for hybrids with battery banks.
- Smaller cable size for high-voltage hybrid systems offers additional weight savings.
- Less routine engine maintenance.
- Redundancies in propulsion systems of parallel hybrids.

Cons:
- Fairly expensive and complex.
- More failure points (inverters, controllers).
- Difficult to repair in remote locations.
- Trading mechanical inefficiencies for electric ones reduces or negates gains.
- Weight penalty for large and powerful battery banks (in hybrids).

Meanwhile, the push is on to develop the next generation hybrid system. Calder initiated the Hybrid Marine (HYMAR) research project that is funded by the European Union to develop an optimized and fully integrated hybrid-electric system for commercial and recreational vessels up to 72 feet. "Newer battery technologies have much lower losses (lithium is close to 0%), and if you expand the perspective to look at the cost of the rest of the energy used by the boat, you find a hybrid can meet these needs with savings on the order of several hundred percent," Calder described the outlook. "There are no systems in the marketplace, which are user friendly, and almost all are less efficient than conventional inboard diesels, but at a much higher price. And, of course, there have been lots of problems in the field." Besides tweaking efficiencies, the project also wants to develop new products and a design for a keel-mounted hybrid drive that builders can purchase as a bolt-on unit. Calder's partners in this undertaking are several companies and institutions, including Bosch Engineering from Germany, Malö Yachts from Sweden, Steyr Motors from Austria, but also Dave Tether who was happy about getting "the financial and research support we need to expand into larger vessels and important new markets." Calder spread optimism in his blog: "I believe we are on the cusp of a series of systems revolutions that will result in more changes to our boat systems than anything we have seen in the last 25 years. Integration of alternative energy sources is the key to making hybrid technology viable in boats."

Will it be easy? "If we had had any idea what we were getting into, we would have refused to build this boat," admitted Hans Leander, a designer at Malö Yachts, the company that built Calder's research vessel. Added Calder: "I've been feeling a bit the same way: we are uncomfortably close to the bleeding edge, rather than the leading edge, of new technology."

SOURCES:
Electric Marine Propulsion: www.electricmarinepropulsion.org
Glacier Bay: www.glacierbay.com
HYMAR: www.hybrid-marine.co.uk
Lagoon Catamarans: www.cata-lagoon.com
Malö Yachts: www.maloyachts.com
Steyr Motors North America: www.steyr-motorsna.com

Electric propulsion

What if there were no fumes, no noise, no gas and no oil? Wouldn't the world be a better place? Actually yes, and sailors already know this better than most everybody else. Except for those moments when they give in to the urge of pushing the starter button that brings to life the iron genny. But what if the iron genny is an electric genny that doesn't add CO_2 and hydrocarbons to the atmosphere? Will electric propulsion become convenient enough in cars and boats to help save us from ourselves and global warming? On the surface, electricity looks great. It's clean, it's ubiquitous and it is the epitome of progress. However, the dirty secret lurks upstream. "There is perhaps no greater act of denial in modern life than sticking a plug into an electric outlet," Corey Powell wrote in the New

York Times' review of the book *Big Coal* by Jeff Goodell. "Fully sanitized of any hint of its origins, it pours out of the socket almost like magic . . . Goodell breaks the spell with a single number: 20. That's how many pounds of coal each person in the United States consumes, on average, every day to keep the electricity flowing. Despite its outdated image, coal generates half of our electricity, far more than any other source. As Goodell puts it, 'our shiny white iPod economy is propped up by dirty black rocks.'"

It's not just the appliances and electronic gadgets that are ratcheting up the thirst for electricity worldwide. Charging boat batteries at home or at the marina dock also shifts the pollution to the utility companies that produce electricity that mostly comes from dirty black rocks. So how does electric propulsion for boats make sense? The same way hybrid makes sense enhancing the experience without noise and spewing noxious exhaust in the presence of those who seek recreation. "Motoring across an ocean is a silly and short-lived concept," said Jason Russell, CEO of Soldinav, a small company that markets in-and outboard electric motors for sailboat applications. "I anticipate a huge influx of boat builders embracing their clients' desires for electric propulsion." His hopes rest with manufacturers who want to add electric options to their offerings and the re-powering market with inboard systems that are rated at 4 KW and 8 KW, respectively (7KW and 14 KW peak) to fit popular standard motor mounts, such as the Atomic 4 and Westerbeke 30 diesels. Real-life performance of a properly-sized inboard electric motor, he said, can be expected to provide "a range of up to 40 miles on a Ranger 27 at an average speed of four knots."

Russell maintained that 80 percent of sailors' needs are covered by cheap and ubiquitous lead-acid batteries, but that is certain to change, because lithium-ion, lithium-manganese, and lithium-polymer batteries reduce weight and promise more speed and/or more range, which are all desirable qualities. The challenge is finding the golden compromise between what's possible and what's affordable. One of the undeniable arguments for e-power is the instantaneously available torque at all rpm, starting at zero all the way up. Inexperienced skippers, Russell said, "love the linear torque and the agility of their boat under electric power when docking." Another plus is the reduced maintenance since there are no fuel issues (as with biodiesel or ethanol), oil changes or mechanical parts that wear out. That's a lot of upside. So why hasn't e-power caught on *en masse*? "I used to own an Olson 30 and put about 8,000 miles on it," said Chuck Hawley, West Marine's vice president of product information. "Most of the time an electric outboard like the ones that are available today would have done the job for me, getting in and out of the marina dock. But if you want to go farther, you will notice that it takes an awful lot of batteries to store enough energy to go the distance. You realize how much energy a gallon of gas or diesel really packs. It gives you a lot of push."

A lot of push is the pitch of Torqeedo, a German outfit that manufactures electric outboards of various sizes and power levels. Like cars and other products made in Germany, these motors are not short on engineering. Features like integrated lithium-manganese batteries, brushless digital motors, rare-earth magnets, large 12-inch props, variable reverse gear, and the ability to set a desired run time have netted Torqeedo several industry awards. It's a business of building a better mousetrap with better components and smarter electronics. The company claims that its motors can turn 44 percent or more of electric energy input into propulsive power, whereas combustion engines hover around 20 percent. "We started developing the technology in 2004 with an eye on optimizing efficiency," said Torqeedo's U.S. sales manager Steve Trkla, who also insisted that Torqeedo is not a trolling-motor company, but targets the market of small outboards between two and 9.9 horsepower that are most often used on kayaks, dinghies and small keelboats. At the Pacific Strictly Sail Expo in Oakland, he demonstrated the Torqeedo Travel 801, a foldable electric outboard that weighs about 25 pounds, including battery.

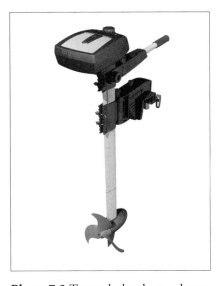

Photo 7.3 Torqeedo has been advancing the cause of electric outboards with efficient components, better batteries, and sophisticated controllers. The company targets the market for small-boat propulsion. *Torqeedo*

But the centerpiece of any electric motor is the battery. Lead-acid batteries still are widely used because they're cheap, well understood, and readily available. They still have their places and qualities, as performance numbers show, but in high-energy applications they are forced into retreat by the emergence of lithium-based batteries, which are the new smart kids on the block. They have plenty of talent, but they are not cheap and require some TLC:

- Energy density: Modern high-power batteries are lithium based because of the higher energy density. This means that lithium battery banks can either be much smaller than lead-acid or AGM banks of the same capacity. Or if weight and space were of no importance (which is unlikely on a pleasure boat), they could be of equal weight but vastly higher capacity.
- Resistance to high current: Conventional batteries can only provide a fraction of their nominal capacity for the loads in the power range of electric outboards.
- Charge stability: Lithium-based batteries maintain their charge, so storage does not affect them as much as lead-acid batteries, which can hold only a fraction of their charge for a longer period.
- Temperature stability: Not so important in Florida, but whoever had to call AAA for a jump on an icy winter morning when the car refused to start will appreciate a battery that performs in cold weather.
- Safety: Torqeedo claims that lithium manganese cells are the safest of the lithium batteries, which require elaborate safety mechanisms to prevent overcharging, overheating, or mechanical damage.
- Useful life: Lithium-ion batteries lose capacity with age (approximately 4 percent per year). They don't have a memory effect like nickel-cadmium batteries, but their lifetime depends on the storage temperature and the charge state. Torqeedo recommends discharging the battery before storing it for a longer period and keeping it in a cool place.

How would a fictitious grudge match between old- and new-style batteries end? It's not a blowout, that's for sure. According to Torqeedo's literature, the range of a 1.5-ton 29-foot Dragon keelboat powered by the Travel 801 motor with integrated 29.6 V/10 Ah lithium manganese battery varies from nine nautical miles at ca. 1.5 knots to 1.9 nm at 4.5 knots. Getting more miles means bringing a fully charged backup battery. By comparison, the same motor with two 12 V/ 80 Ah lead batteries will push a 620-pound 16-foot rowboat more than 83 nm at 2.2 knots and 9 nm at 4.5 knots. On a Dragon the range varies from 48.1 nm at 1.3 knots to 8.2 nm at 4.1 knots. Torqeedo's model range also includes the Ultralight, a tiny and fully submersible kayak outboard, a smaller and lighter version of the Travel model, and the top-of-the-line Cruise with integrated GPS, which the company says delivers the thrust power that's equivalent to a 9.9-hp gasoline outboard motor. Company data for a 2.6-ton 40-foot Skerry cruiser that is powered by the Cruise 2.0 model, show ranges from 10 to 165 nm at speeds decreasing from 5 to 1.5 knots and run times from two to 110 hours on two 12 V/200 Ah lead batteries.

With so many avenues, models and options to choose from, it looks like advanced electric outboards could become an alternative to fossil fuel technology. What's holding them back is purchase price. "A Honda gasoline 2 hp 4-stroke costs less than $1,000, while the Torqeedo Travel 801 lists for $1,699," Trkla noted. However, over the span of the electric motor's useful life, the savings in maintenance and gasoline should more than make up for the differential. Regarding the black rocks: The percentage of "dirty electricity" varies by geography and is hard to predict with the complex electricity trading schemes that cover peak demands. Ask your utility about the sources and if they offer a clean energy option. For a surcharge, you can buy electricity that comes from renewable sources, i.e. solar, wind or hydroelectric power plants. Some thoughts to sort through before committing to e-power:

Pros:
- Clean, no exhaust, no discharge of unburned oil or fuel
- Quiet
- No or low maintenance (i.e. no oil changes)
- Efficient, no mechanical losses and wear (i.e. transmission gears)
- No break-in period
- No fuel issues (i.e. compatibility with ethanol or "wet" fuel)

◆ Portability, compactness
◆ Instant, linear torque for easy and precise maneuvering
◆ Can use renewable energy sources for battery charging

Cons:
◆ Range/speed ratio
◆ Few electric motors have integrated waterproof batteries, which means added complexity of keeping them and their cable connectors dry
◆ Conventional charging requires a dock connection or carrying the battery home
◆ Electricity from the grid often is generated by burning coal
◆ Price

SOURCES:
SolidNav: www.solidnav.com
Torqeedo: www.torqeedo.com

Renewable Energy

One of the underlying principles of sustainable sailing is the use of renewable energy sources that can provide electrical energy without combustion power while a vessel is under way. Each technology has its advantages and limitations, but any combination of them is likely to carry the day, provided that the energy household is well managed and not weighed down by energy hogs such as air conditioning or refrigeration. "I get all my power from renewable energy," circumnavigator Cap'n Fatty Goodlander offered when I asked him for advice on going green when cruising the Big Blue. He's one of thousands of cruisers who tap into free and clean energy sources to keep the lights on. "I have a Kiss wind generator, which I love. It is very efficient, however only over a narrow range of conditions, i.e. from 14 to 21 knots, the typical spectrum of wind speeds you see in the Caribbean. Back in the 1970s I bought a solar module for $1,200, a fortune at the time. But 25 years later when I finally gave it away, it still worked. That's a good return on investment and works out to fractions of pennies for each kilowatt hour generated. When people ask me if they should install solar or wind generators, I tell them they'd have to do both. Never use wind without solar."

Renewable energy can also come from the water by converting the kinetic energy of a moving boat into electricity with a generator that's towed behind the boat. It's a technology that's been around for a while, and it uses an impeller that spins in the current while the boat merrily sails its course. Set it and forget it, and enjoy free electricity, a collateral benefit of a sustainable practice. Fuel cells hold the promise of collateral benefits as they convert fuel like hydrogen or methanol into electricity through electrochemical conversion, not through combustion power. That's a clean and quiet alternative or complement to battery technology. The production of fuel can be green as well, by using biomass and electrolysis that is powered by sun and/or wind energy. We'll meet an engineer from Canada who's done it for a couple of small boats with off-the-shelf parts and we'll look across the pond where fuel cells are not just surfacing in RVs and production boats, but now come with the necessary fuel infrastructure. Perhaps the best story about fuel cells is that this technology seemed too utopian and expensive a few years ago for use in cars or boats, but here we are with actual solutions—not just products—that can be bought "over the counter."

Solar power

How far solar can go as a mode of boat propulsion was demonstrated in 2007, by SUN21, a Swiss-built 45-foot catamaran that made a 7,000-mile journey from Basel, Switzerland via Seville, Spain across the Atlantic to New York under solar power alone. It had a 700 sq. ft, "sun roof" with two 5-KW photovoltaic modules and used batteries to power two 8-KW electric motors that propelled the boat to a cruising speed of 5 to 6 knots. But for the intents and purposes of sailors, solar power is used to provide juice for the batteries, which in turn power various devices on board. And there are plenty of advantages: It uses the sun, the most abundant energy source, so it's clean. There are no moving parts, so it is quiet. If properly designed and installed, hardly any service is required, save for the cleaning of the solar panels. Since sunlight is distributed anywhere in the world at no cost, photovoltaic electrical systems (PV) and solar water heaters are central components to micro generation, which leads to grid independence. But the dark side of solar is relatively low efficiency and high cost, which is a bit surprising given the history of the technology. French physicist Alexandre-Edmond Becquerel discovered the photovoltaic effect in 1839, and in 1883 American inventor Charles Fritts is said to have built the first solar cell by coating selenium with a thin layer of gold. Starting in the 1950s, space exploration pushed the development of solar cells to power satellites and other spacecraft such as the International Space Station.

But there are other challenges, too: Depending on energy needs, a large number (and area) of PV cells are necessary to generate enough electricity. That's a conundrum on sailboats that have few good spots to mount them, so they won't be shaded by the rig and the sails, which is highly detrimental for their efficiency. One tiny bit of shade anywhere on a solar module kills most of its generation power. "It's like pinching one inch of a water hose, which renders the rest of it useless," one solar expert explained the problem.

Solar cells produce electricity either through silicon crystals or thin chemical films. For crystalline cells silicon is refined and puri-fied before it gets sliced into thin wafers and prepped with chemi-cals. When exposed to light, one side of the wafer produces a surplus, the other side a deficit of electrons while a voltage difference between the two sides occurs. How much electricity solar cells cre-ate, depends on their size and efficiency and how much sun they get. By connecting 30 or 36 solar cells manufacturers produce modules, which is what shows up on houses and boats.

What technology works best, depends on the energy needs, the size of the boat and the tolerance of ungainly superstructures by the skipper. Multicrystalline panels are the most efficient, but also the most difficult to install, because they tend to be heavy and cum-bersome. Many cruisers attach solar panels to the top of a hard dodger (if they have one) or they have to build an ugly arch on the stern to mount the panels free and clear from obstructions and shade. That also keeps the panels cool, which is important to pre-vent voltage from dropping. However, putting weight high up and/or far aft makes sailors cringe, as it will result in roly-poly downwind passages and a boat that drags the stern. That's quite effective in slowing things down.

One solution for shading problems are shade-tolerant modules that feature so-called by-pass diodes, which can be applied to each cell or to strings of cells, so a little shade in one corner won't render the whole module useless. The other option is to use thin-film sili-con panels, which are light, flexible and stowable, but only about 50 percent as effective. They can be contoured to the shape of the deck and do a good job in producing electricity when it's overcast. West

Marine maintains that these panels are OK to "float" or trickle charge a battery.

"Solar panels on boats face several challenges," said Immanuel Moebius, managing director of the German company Sunplastics, which produces solar modules that are embedded in plastic resins to save weight and make them suitable for mobile applications. "Modules have to be light and strong, so they can be mounted in areas where the crew works and steps on them. They also have to be integrated with the other components of the onboard electrical system." Standard glass modules, Moebius said, are heavy and fragile; thin-film modules are not very efficient, which means that they'd need more surface area than boats normally offer. His company therefore developed Sunovation, a hybrid technology that uses crystalline modules, which are embedded in layers of clear plastic and gel. "These modules are step-resistant and weigh only half as much as common crystalline modules," Moebius explained. They also can be molded to the deck shape of the boat and color matched." There are ways to make more power from smaller modules, but that's a costly proposition, because it requires high-efficiency cells that are made from very expensive and pure materials, like copper, indium, gallium or selenium. They also can be equipped with a layer of Fresnel lenses that distribute the light to the cells.

Solar panels are rated in watts or kilowatts or in watt-hours or kilowatt-hours per day, which is helpful to determine the size and the number of the panels that can meet a boat's power needs. Moebius estimated that one square meter (roughly 10.7 square feet) of reasonably efficient solar cells produces 100 to 130 W of electricity per hour, but cautions that the pattern and the geometry of the cells influence this calculation. On a good sunny day, a 100 W panel that has five hours of full exposure to the sun can produce approximately 500 watt-hours of energy, minus 20 to 30 percent that get lost during charging and/or inverting. A laptop computer that consumes on average 75 watts per hour, Moebius calculated, could run for approximately five hours with the electricity that is produced by a 10-square foot solar panel on a decent day. That does not include losses incurred by shading, improper angle of the panels facing the sun (meaning less than 90-degrees) and overheating.

There are many other tricks to make solar work on a boat, but it needs to tie in with the rest of the existing system. Adding solar to the power mix of a sailboat is commendable but it might be worthwhile to consult with experts who can help figure out the parameters. Above all, potential solar users should remember to keep a realistic outlook. "Boaters usually overestimate what solar panels can produce and underestimate their electrical needs," West Marine warns. "Make a list of the appliances on your boat, get the amperage (Amps = Watts ÷ Voltage) and estimate the operating hours to get weekly amp hours for each device. You can then create an estimate of your electrical budget and size your system correctly." With this perspective Goodlander's tactic of combining various energy sources for battery charging makes perfect sense. But it wouldn't be as effective if he hadn't eliminated air conditioning and refrigeration, the two most power-hungry appliances on a boat. While most probably can survive a sailing trip without AC, refrigeration would be nice. Perhaps it's time to invest in a rally cool cooler, one of these industrial-style models that are heavily insulated and keep food and beer cold for extended periods with wet and/or dry ice. Regardless, reducing the demand will make the energy budget look a lot less daunting and make solar power more appealing because it will cover a much bigger percentage of the on-board energy needs. Some points to ponder about solar energy:

Pros:
- Quiet
- Clean
- Provides energy independence
- Needs no fuel or lubrication
- Low or no maintenance (set it and forget it)
- Long-lived (solar panels have no mechanical parts to wear out)
- A visible statement for sustainable practices

Cons:
- Space requirements
- Shading issues on sailboats
- Mounting options
- Efficiency
- Cost

SOURCES:
West Marine: www.westmarine.com
Sunplastics: www.sunplastics.de
Transatlantic 21: www.transatlantic21.org
Solar Sailor: www.solarsailor.com

Wind generators

"How can you prepare for a cloudy day? The answer is blowing in the wind." This bon mot on the home page of the Air Breeze wind generator Web site hints at the strengths of the technology: Picking up the slack of solar when it's less than sunny. What it doesn't say is that wind generators actually harness a byproduct of the sun's energy.

When I was cruising with my parents in the 1970s we made our own electricity with a small wind generator that was mounted on the cabin top. Marinas with convenient shore power outlets were still a few decades away on the Croatian coast. The idea to get light from the wind was good, but the result was unimpressive. When it worked—if it worked at all—the little turbine produced earsplitting noise and erratic charging performance, so it spent most of its time dismantled in the lazarette. That limited our electric autonomy, but that was no big deal since we sailed most of the time anyway and that was how it was supposed to be. It emphasized the rustic character of the undertaking, but that was fine too, because we enjoyed the lifestyle that was so different from the one on terra firma and its associated chores. Besides, it made us appreciate the conveniences of home a little more. Dad spent more time worrying about making the boat move well than loading it down with gadgets and complex equipment that kept them running. "It's a sailboat," he used to say. "If you want light on deck, there are gas and kerosene lamps." The only devices that needed a little bit of battery power were the cabin and the running lights. But since we rarely sailed at night, it was not a big concern.

But times have changed. Comfort and convenience have replaced boat camping, and most cruising boats have much bigger energy demands. Wind generation helps to meet the electricity needs on thousands of cruising boats, especially those that need energy independence for long-distance voyages. Contrary to the giant commercial wind turbines that are now dotting the landscape and the shores, the small-diameter turbines on sailboats operate at high rpm when the breeze is up, which can be a noisy nuisance. They have to deal with pesky problems, such as damage from over-speeding, over-heating alternator components, or putting out unregulated voltage that could damage battery systems. Creative low-tech solutions include turning the turbine away from the wind and tethering it, manual brakes, internal friction devices, centrifugal air brakes or feathering propeller blades.

Modern wind generators are smaller, smarter, lighter and bear only little resemblance to the contraption we grappled with nearly four decades years ago. Advanced models feature microprocessor-based internal regulators and torque controls that track output power to throttle the rpm as necessary. This reduces the racket from the blades and the whining of the alternator and prevents damage from over-speeding and over-charging. Blade design also improved, so the effective wind range is wider, which means the generator starts to produce appreciable power at lighter breezes and still keeps cranking out the watts in controlled fashion when it blows with more than 25 knots. The Air-Breeze Web site specifies start-up wind speed with 6 mph and a rated power of 200W at 28 mph, which is just about the upper end of the wind speed on a nice day in the Trades. Survival wind speed, the specs say, is 110 mph. The guidance given for the monthly energy production at an average wind speed of 12 mph is 38 kWh. That's pretty good, but limitations remain.

Product literature points out that doubling the wind speed increases actual energy

Photo 8.1 The DuoGen wind/tow generator is a two-trick pony that can use either wind or forward motion as energy source to generate electricity. *DuoGen*

by the factor of eight, so the energy is wind velocity cubed. How much of this energy can be harnessed is subject to debate, but long-time cruisers calculate with 20 to 25 percent, slightly better than crystalline solar panels. Wind generators work in conjunction with photovoltaic installations, but most likely they will need a different regulator. They also have a switch that disconnects the turbine from the battery bank to prevent damage from over charging. So the technology got smarter, but also more complex. Therefore the suggestion "Never use wind without solar." And vice versa.

Pros:
* No emissions
* Harnesses free energy
* Works day and night
* Takes up less space than solar panels
* Can be mounted out of the way, mostly on a pole at the stern
* Can be very productive within operative wind range

Cons:
* Noise, especially with older generator models
* Mechanical losses
* Wear and tear
* Might require extra charge regulator
* Aesthetics

SOURCES:
AirBreeze: www.airbreeze.com
Kiss: www.kissenergy.com
Southeast Marine Services: www.semarine.com
West Marine: www.westmarine.com

Tow generation

If sustainability is a result of efficiency we have to tip our hat to the wind three times. First, for pushing the boat along; second, for turning the wind generator to produce power; and third, for being the source of kinetic energy that also can be turned into electricity. For a long time, this kinetic energy has been harnessed with generators that are towed behind on a long cable. These generators "are suitable for all sailboats and sailing speeds in blue and coastal waters," promises the Seatech Web site for the AquaGen tow generator. "They can provide sufficient power to satisfy all power requirements whilst under sail." The concept is straight forward: An impeller that can be fitted with blades of different sizes is towed behind the boat and travels up to 10 feet under water. It is connected to a generator that is strapped to the pushpit, which in turn is connected to the battery bank vie a charge regulator. It's quiet, it works whenever the vessel moves, and it's pretty reliable as long as the impeller stays under water and connected to the boat.

As discussed earlier, the concept of tow generation becomes "regeneration" in a hybrid system, with the notable difference that hybrid propulsion uses the vessel's existing propeller as an "impeller," while tow generators put another impeller in the water, which necessarily increases drag and reduces sailing performance. AquaGen's specifications talk about a continuous output of 11 amps at 8 knots of boat speed and 16 amps at 12 knots of boat speed with the larger model. This sounds quite optimistic for real-life conditions on loaded-down small to mid-sized cruising boats that commonly top out at seven, maybe eight knots.

Photo 8.2 The DuoGen wind/tow generator in action. *DuoGen*

Owing to the fact that wind and tow generators can complement each other, the UK company Eclectic Energy Ltd manufactures the DuoGen, a combined water/wind generator that can alternate between the two modes without tools. Electric Energy Ltd. claims that the incurred loss of speed with the DuoGen deployed is less than 0.15 knots while it produces anywhere from 8 to 16 amps (or 100 to 200W) at boat speeds from 6 to 8 knots. Wind generation numbers are slightly less than that, ranging from 40W to 150W at wind speeds between 10 and 20 knots. Mounted at the stern of the vessel, the main advantages of this generator combo are compactness, quick deployment and recovery, plus no hassle with a cable in the water.

The argument for a combined wind/tow generator points out that dedicated wind generators need a lot of breeze to be effective. "This is of limited use to most yachtsmen who generally avoid high wind speeds, and do most of their sailing in more benign Beaufort numbers," DuoGen said. "This is when most power is actually consumed aboard a yacht and, by definition, when most power is required to replace it." Bolting the unit to the stern rather than towing it 100 feet behind the boat has other advantages, because no rope means there is much less drag and the impeller can't foul or jump out of the water. It's also less likely to get bitten off by a hungry shark. Attached to a mounting bracket and fitted to a yaw arm, the water impeller is prevented from resurfacing by an adjustable diving plane. It remains protected by the vessel's keel and rudder as it operates in the top two feet of water, within the same wave as the yacht. Most of the system's weight is at deck level, and switching from water to wind mode doesn't require special tools, changing electrical connections or repositioning the alternator. Both turbines can be used interchangeably and can be disassembled and stowed when not in use.

On long downwind passages in traditional boats that have displacement hulls the apparent wind will diminish, which is a strike against a wind generator, while boat speed is relatively constant and high, favoring the water mode. Easy deployment, DuoGen says, makes it more likely for the crew to use the unit even on shorter trips. Swinging on the hook in a good tidal current (2+ knots), the generator can be operated in water mode, which is quiet and works independent from daylight.

Tow generation adds another option that helps cutting back on combustion power. However, the manufacturers' performance claims tend to be optimistic and loosely defined, so the prudent customer will get clarification about the collected data and ask for reference customers who have used the products in real-life conditions. If a generator delivers 10 amps at 10 knots of boat speed but your vessel only does six or seven, you have to adjust your expectations ,and your energy budget accordingly.

SOURCES:
AquaGen: www.seateach.com/aquagen.asp
DuoGen: www.duogen.co.uk

Fuel cells

Long before the U.S. administration began touting this technology as deliverance from oil addiction, the German company MTU Friedrichshafen introduced No. 1, an experimental propulsion system for sailboats based on gel batteries and fuel cells. MTU's Cool-Cell system drew hydrogen from a tank and oxygen from the air to generate electricity. The emission was only water, so it was clean, but it faced formidable drawbacks, such as limited range and exorbitant cost. That was in 2004 and the intervening years have seen progress that has brought fuel cells into the recreational market.

Fuel cells come in many different varieties. They are electro-chemical conversion devices that produce electricity from fuel at the anode and an oxidant at the cathode, which react in the presence of an electrolyte. The reactants flow into the cell and the products of the reaction flow out of it, while the electrolyte remains inside. The difference to batteries, which store electrical energy chemically in a thermodynamically closed system, is that fuel cells are thermodynamically open, because they need to be fueled with a reactant. Perhaps best known is the hydrogen fuel cell that uses hydrogen as fuel and oxygen as oxidant. It works well, but requires a lot of expertise to be handled properly.

Marshall Duffield, president of the Duffy Electric Boat Co., a U.S. builder of electric boats, believes that hydrogen fuel cells eventually will take zero-emission boats much farther than batteries can. "We have a 4-kW experimental fuel-cell system for our Duffy 30

Photo 8.3 A dash of Yankee pioneer spirit tweaked an old Evinrude outboard with a Minn Kota drive that's powered by electricity from a hydrogen fuel cell. The sustainable concept also includes solar panels (foreground). It's one of Jim Harrington's solutions that are built from off-the-shelf components. *Jim Harrington*

model that can carry 23 people and does 7.5 knots," he said. "Our next step is producing hydrogen on demand from sea water, so we don't have to lug it around in a humongous tank." Duffy thought it'll be viable, but conceded that the cost was off the charts. "Like with space exploration, the government needs to step in and help fund the development of fuel-cell technology," he said.

Jim Harrington, an electronics and mechanical product designer in Victoria, BC, Canada, proved that progress is possible without the government or a giant budget. He runs his own company, AGO Environmental Electronics, Ltd., but he's also known as an inventor and a developer of research and exploration equipment in astrophysics, geophysics, and oceanographic applications. As a casual sailor, he's also all too familiar with a diesel's noise and fumes and one day decided he'd had enough. "I said to myself, there has to be a better way and my mind went back to that fuel cell." He became acquainted with this technology back in the 1970s when it helped power NASA's lunar exploration.

First he helped design a hydrogen fuel cell for a bicycle with auxiliary propulsion, then he continued to climb on the learning curve by converting a Minn Kota trolling motor to hydrogen fuel cell propulsion. He clamped it to the shaft of an Evinrude outboard that normally powers his bilge keeler, SLOOP JIM D. "I put to sea for the boat's maiden run and successfully completed a two-mile trip that started and finished with hydrogen. What a beautiful ride it was, especially the portions while under fuel cell drive. The boat slipped through the water almost totally quiet, except for the occasional puff of water vapor coming out of the fuel cell's exhaust." To fuel this experience, Harrington obtained hydrogen that was made through solar-powered electrolysis as opposed to getting it from a petrochemical refinery.

"We put zero carbon into the environment while using the hydrogen fuel cell. Our byproducts are electricity, pure water, heat and small amounts of unused hydrogen during venting. Absolutely nothing to harm the environment." For developing Canada's first fuel cell powered sailboat, the alumni association of Harrington's alma mater, Loyalist College, in Belleville, Ontario, honored him with the 2008 Ontario Premier's Award for technology, but he won't rest on his laurels. He proceeded to convert an old 4-hp outboard to electric/fuel cell operation and thought of ways to use the warm air that is being discharged by a fuel cell. He connected a simple oil-filled radiator to an inverter that he then hooked up to a fuel cell. The result was a zero-emission electrical heater for the house. Hydrogen takes more energy to produce than can be obtained by burning it, but if that energy is clean, free and renewable the equation could work. Harrington believes that electrolysis with solar cells could produce hydrogen all summer long so it could be stored in a tank. Come the cold season, it's ready to provide the electricity to heat the house.

Hydrogen is the most abundant chemical element in the universe, but it is complex to handle safely. It is explosive when mixed with air in high quantities. In its pure form it is an asphyxiant that displaces oxygen and it can affect metals, all of which has critics concerned. "The Hindenburg effect has come to our attention," replied Ian Soutar, a partner in Harrington's project. "The only dangerous part of hydrogen is that it is odorless, therefore you need a detector." These devices are not expensive, yet they detect hydrogen in low, non-explosive concentrations and set off an alarm before matters get critical. "Hydrogen will rise rapidly and leave the area," Soutar explained. "It is actually difficult for hydrogen to build up from a slight leak since [it] has a small atom and sneaks out of places that would trap air. A roof vent will keep a boat safe." Besides explosion, he conceded, hydrogen can act as an asphyxiant that displaces oxygen in tight spaces. "People can die from the lack of oxygen in extreme leaks, [but] this does not usually happen since most hydrogen work areas have a roof vent and alarms that will go off well in advance of a gas buildup."

What Harrington and Soutar accomplished with off-the-shelf components is remarkable, no doubt. The next step in the fuel-cell game is putting it on a production scale and integrating it with the necessary infrastructure. It's a big task that seeks to level the advantage of grid electricity that already has millions of outlets in place in homes, offices and marinas. Frauscher and two Austrian technology companies, Fronius and Bitter, have taken the leap with the Future Project Hydrogen. It was introduced in Austria in April of 2009 and showcased a fuel-cell powered production boat and a hydrogen-filled metal cartridge that can be replaced by the user. "Instead of docking, plugging in and waiting for hours for the batteries to get recharged, all you need is swap out the container and off you go," said Stefan Frauscher. "It's a three-minute affair." But equally interesting was the collaboration between technology providers and local municipalities to establish the principle of a closed-loop system that includes fuel supply, and the distribution and the refilling of hydrogen cartridges.

Like Harrington, Frauscher is convinced that hydrogen as the better energy storage option could supplement batteries in electric boats. In addition to drastically shorter refueling times, the hydrogen cell also yields about twice the operation range of a set of standard AGM batteries. Frauscher also likes the hydrogen package for reducing by more than 300 pounds the weight of a comparable battery installation in his Riviera 600 runabout. The boat's seven-gallon tank is filled at 350 bar (ca. 5,000 psi), which packs seven cubic meters (247 cubic feet) of hydrogen. That's good for approximately 50 miles at cruising speed. "We plan to offer two refueling systems," said Michael Schubert, the project manager at Fronius, the company that developed the fuel-cell for the Frauscher boat. "One

Photo 8.4 Swapping out a hydrogen cartridge like the battery of an electronic gadget: That's the idea behind the future project Hydrogen, that promotes hydrogen-powered boats and the infrastructure for producing and delivering the fuel to the consumer. *Frauscher*

is a cartridge swap-out, like it has been used for propane gas bottles; the other is a dockside fueling station that has hydrogen instead of gasoline pumps." The idea is to market an integrated concept, not just a boat. "Fuel cells are suitable for the mainstream market if the infrastructure is there," Frauscher said. "To get there, we have to market it to fleet customers, such as rentals, municipalities and resorts who run multiple boats and use one centralized supply point."

Independence from internal combustion and the tether of limited battery capacities is the pitch of German manufacturer SFC Smart Fuel Cells AG who promises "unlimited freedom" for sailors who want to drop the hook anywhere and still have enough power to run their onboard appliances. "With the EFOY fuel cell you have your own power supply with you, anytime anywhere—ultra-reliable, quiet and maintenance-free." The system, which operates on methanol and won the DAME award, consists of fuel cells with a rated output from 25 to 65 watts and methanol fuel canisters of 1.3 or 2.6 gallons. The fuel cell connects to the 12V battery that powers the boat's DC house loads. A built-in charge control regulator monitors the battery state and switches the cell on when voltage is low. After recharging, the cell shuts off automatically. SFC says their fuel cell can operate in conjunction with solar panels or wind generators and comes on automatically if the other sources can't keep the battery voltage above 12.3V.

"With more than 12,000 fuel cells sold, our core business is the RV market in Europe," explained Bjoern Ledergerber, spokesman for SFC. "The marine market is not yet as big, but we're making inroads, especially in France." SFC also set up an operation in the U.S. and hopes to work with "a large marine retailer" to market the EFOY technology to boaters. "Methanol is a liquid and as such it is easier to handle than hydrogen," Ledergerber outlined the advantages of this versatile yet toxic alcohol, which is used for making chemicals, plastics, plywood, paints, explosives, textiles but also the gasoline additive MTBE and biodiesel. Methanol is relatively cheap, but mostly sold as a byproduct of natural gas production. Strictly speaking it is not part of a renewable cycle, although it is also possible to generate it from biomass (i.e. manure).

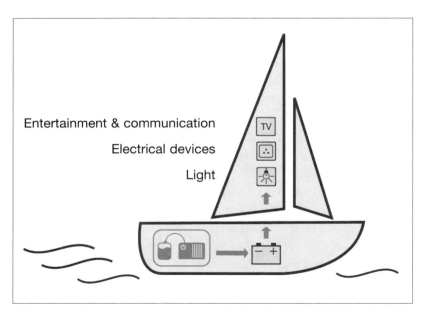

Photo 8.5 Methanol + fuel cell + battery = power for a boat's electric house loads. *EFOY*

One of the challenges for SFC is to expand the distribution network that one day also should compare to the exchange and refill stations of propane gas canisters. Another one is convincing boaters to fork over between 2,000 and 4,000 Euros for the fuel cell and controller plus 25 Euros for a 2.6-gallon canister of methanol, which should suffice to power the onboard appliances on a medium-sized cruising boat for three to four weeks, according to Ledergerber.

As technology evolves, SFC will introduce fuel cells that can charge lithium-ion batteries and not just lead-acid AGMs that are still the standard on most boats and RVs.

Despite their complexity, fuel cells are making inroads as alternatives to electric propulsion systems that rely purely on battery power. Eventually, they might show up in production sailboats, too. The technology, although still expensive, has decreased dramatically in price. "A fuel-cell boat that costs 150,000 Euros today would have cost 1.5 million four years ago," Frauscher said, conceding that the success of this technology will depend on the creation of a convenient infrastructure and reliable supplies.

SOURCES:
Ago Environmental: www.agoenvironmental.com
Frauscher: www.frauscherboats.com
Fronius: www.fronius.com
Future Project Hydrogen: www.futureprojecthydrogen.com
SFC/EFOY: www.efoy.com
MTU: www.mtu-online.com

9

Heads or Travails?

Whenever toilet etiquette on boats becomes the topic, there's the inevitable awkward moment. It's icky, it's personal and nobody likes to discuss it in public. Yet there are stubborn misconceptions and bad practices that seek to minimize the problem of pump-and-dump practices, which have become a public health hazard in many places, even in formerly pristine cruising grounds. "It's happened for thousands of years. Dumping garbage and sewage into the sea has a long tradition," I was told by people who are smart enough to know better. "What comes from the boats is a tiny fraction of what's dumped by cities," was another excuse that frequently was used to explain the status quo. And lastly: "They didn't have the money to build the infrastructure and people either don't have holding tanks on their boats or they don't use them."

Over the last 40 years, the number of sailors and boats have increased exponentially almost anywhere. To paraphrase Goodlander's observation: Where there was one boat there now are 100. This means that the amount of sewage pumped into the water increased exponentially too, putting ecosystems under more pressure.

Raw sewage (or black water) contains microbial pathogens that pose a serious health threat to swimmers, snorkelers and divers and all forms of marine life, if discharged into any body of water untreated. As filter feeders, shellfish are especially susceptible to pathogens that can cause paralytic shellfish poisoning if ingested by humans. Sewage also reduces the oxygen in the water, which is another strike against aquatic wildlife and it may contain suspended solids that could blanket species or reduce light penetration at greater depth. Discharged sewage can produce an excess of nutrients and pathogens in the water column. In poorly flushed areas, i.e. bays and inlets, this fosters the growth of so-called macro-algae and the phytoplankton that can pose a health risk to humans while taking away oxygen from bottom-dwelling species. Localized effects on coral reefs, for instance, include reduced biodiversity, less coral cover and suppressed coral growth.

Additives are used to break down, disinfect and deodorize waste in portable toilets (which are popular on smaller boats) but they contain chlorine, formaldehyde, ammonium and zinc. Needless to say, that's another dose of toxins to marine life if dumped in large quantities. That's why I still feel guilty about my gaffe from decades ago. The short of this messy story is: The smaller the body of water and the larger the quantities of raw sewage and chemicals pumped into it, the greater the impact on water quality and aquatic life. The most practical and cost-effective solution to this problem is to take your poop offshore, three miles or more from the nearest coast or island. Discharged into open water, the sauce is diluted and dispersed by wind and currents, which greatly lessens the impact. The regulations issued by the Great Barrier Reef Marine Park Authority require vessels with holding tanks to retain sewage on board and discharge it at least a third of a mile away from reefs. On the Web site, the authority says it is "encouraging the development of pump-out facilities to allow for collection and treatment of ship-sourced sewage, and has developed guidelines for best environmental construction of marina facilities to include pump-out facilities."

If all this sounds onerous, consider the lot of outdoor enthusiasts such as backpackers or kayakers, who spend extended periods in the backcountry or on undeveloped islands. They are supposed to live by a simple rule: Pack it in, pack it out. Not just regular garbage, but also human waste. They use a toilet in a bag, a so-called waste alleviation and gelling bag. These WAG bags consist of a double-bag system, which contains a nontoxic substance called "pooh-powder" that gels waste and neutralizes its odor in the inner bag. When business is done, the outer bag closes with an airtight seal, so the load can be stored until there is a place to dispose of it. The manufacturer says that "waste kits are biodegradable and approved for landfill disposal," so they can be thrown in the regular trash.

Turds vs. turtles

Fish and birds need to go too, right? True, but they do so in smaller quantities, they don't use chemicals and the environment has adapted to their contributions. Besides, they don't have a choice, but sailors do. Now what about land-based run-off and large cruise ships? Both sources are much bigger and more harmful than what recreational boaters dump overboard. That's not a license to dump for sailors, but a motivation for all parties to get together and develop sewage management strategies. West Marine's product advisor for marine sanitation devices puts it bluntly: "Don't operate your head without a means to contain or treat waste on board, and in foreign countries don't pump your waste overboard within 100 yards of the beach. This is harmful to swimmers and those who eat the local fish and shellfish. Just because Caribbean charter boats have little, if any, sewage treatment systems on board doesn't mean it's okay for the rest of us to dump in the otherwise pristine waters regularly used by snorkelers and swimmers." No resort would flourish if sea turtles lose out to fecal matter that's drifting on the tides and gets washed up on the beaches.

Popular charter destinations where large numbers of vessels (sailboats and large cruise ships) congregate during the peak season are exposed to this kind of potty pressure. Charter operators agree that the situation is not ideal, and proclaim to do what's in their power to reduce the impact. "A change in sewage disposal practices has to go hand-in-hand with the improvement of the facilities in the operating areas," stated Peter Cochran, vice president of operations at TUI Marine, the parent company of The Moorings and Sunsail. "Building a pump-out station alone is not enough. To prevent sewage from going back into the water, treatment plants are needed." TUI Marine and other charter firms maintain that most, if not all of their vessels are fitted with holding tanks, which are now standard equipment, but that it's up to the customer to use them properly.

"If I was going to stop working with people who dump sewage, I'd be out of business," quipped Tom Virden of boatbookings.com, a charter broker for luxury vessels. He acknowledged that the industry needs to come together to address pollution issues, but maintained that the challenge is too many small operators and not enough money for retrofits with sophisticated sewage treatment systems.

The good news is that at least in the U.S. some progress is being made. The Clean Vessel Act (CVA) grant program provides money to the states, the District of Columbia and island territories for the construction, renovation, operation, and maintenance of pump-out stations and waste reception facilities for recreational boaters and for educational programs about the importance of proper disposal of sewage. These funds are provided through the Sport Fish Restoration and Boating Trust Fund and come from excise taxes on fishing equipment, motorboat and small engine fuels, import duties, and interest on the fund. Depending on location, the grants cover up to 75 percent of the project costs (in U.S. states and DC) and up to 100 percent in American Samoa, Guam, the Commonwealth of the Northern Mariana Islands and the U.S. Virgin Islands. In 2008, the U.S. Fish and Wildlife Service announced the distribution of more than $13.6 million in grants funding to 27 states for construction and installation of sewage pump-out facilities and floating restrooms, to purchase pump-out boats and for educational programs for recreational boaters.

The law and the Y-valve

Legislation that regulates black water discharge have become more stringent, a trend that is likely to continue. U.S. federal law requires all boats in U.S. waters with permanently installed toilets to have a so-called Marine Sanitation Device (MSD) that is approved by the Coast Guard and either stores human waste until it can be transferred ashore or reduces the coliform count to such low levels that discharged sewage poses no public health hazard. More than three miles from the coast it is legal for boaters to discharge untreated waste overboard, either directly from the toilet or by emptying the holding tank. West Marine for instance recommends systems that are suitable for a dockside pump-out and offshore dumping of the holding tank. Closer to shore, it's only legal to discharge waste that is treated by a Type I or II MSD. Otherwise, it must be contained on board in a holding tank (Type III MSD) and transferred ashore at a pump-out station where it hopefully will get treated thoroughly, not just collected and pumped right back into the water . . .

All non–navigable inland freshwater lakes and the Great Lakes are No Discharge Zones (NDZ), but dumping treated sewage on navigable interstate inland waterways is legal, as long as they are not designated no-discharge zones. Confused? Just remember this. Don't dump any poop, treated or not, in a NDZ. The number of coastal NDZ keeps increasing, which goes hand in hand with the addition of more pump-out facilities funded by the Clean Water Act grant program. Nineteen states have designated No Discharge Zones, while Michigan, New Mexico, Rhode Island and Vermont outlawed discharging sewage in all waters. So sailors who have a toilet on board will, by hook or by crook, become experts in pumping the head either to flush or to empty the holding tank. Some authorities might balk at a Y-valve, which is a piece of plumbing that diverts waste either to the holding tank or directly overboard (so irresponsible operators might call it a Y-not valve).

By law, Y-valves fitted to holding tanks with untreated waste must be secured in the closed position while operating in U.S. waters. BoatU.S. recommends closing the Y-valve and removing its handle or installing a non-releasable wire tie or padlock. If the boat is "headless," consider installing a Coast Guard approved MSD, space permitting. When tied up to a dock, use the shoreside head and remind crew and guests to do the same. Regular head maintenance (including holding tank and plumbing) is unpleasant, but a lot less so than a clogged head or a blown hose clamp on the discharge hose. Invest in the best hose your money can buy to combat potty odors and stay away from aggressive cleaners. Use enzyme deodorizers for holding tanks and portable toilets instead. When you store the boat, remember to pump out before you haul out. If and when the time comes to install or replace the head, there are a few options, so let's compare some toilet systems and comment on their talents:

- Sea toilets: Old style, but no longer acceptable because they dump everything overboard directly and instantly. It's simple, but it's also ugly and illegal inside the three-mile zone.
- Porta Potti: Budget boaters and small-boat sailors know the

pros and cons well: They're cheap, compact and easy to install, because they don't need to be plumbed and usually
won't clog. But the fun stops when it's time to empty out the
holding tank.

- Holding tank with through-deck fittings: That's simple and
  legal, but it works only if the sailing venue has enough accessible pump-out stations and the tank is of decent size so it can
  handle some quantities.
- Holding tank and direct discharge: That's the one with the fa-
  mous Y-valve between toilet and tank. The idea is to divert
  sewage from the toilet overboard where legal and into the
  holding tank close to shore. That system still allows an accidental (or malicious) overboard flush and has no provision
  for emptying the holding tank outside the three-mile limit
  where it's legal. The benefit: If one hose is clogged, at least
  there's an option to go a different route, so to speak, provided
  it doesn't violate the rules of a no-discharge zone.
- Holding tank with multiple discharge options: Here the toilet is flushed into a holding tank every time, but the tank can
  be discharged overboard where legal and pumped out when
  necessary. More complex, but politically correct and environmentally responsible.
- Manual vs. electric heads: On smaller boats, manual heads
  rule, because they tend to be small, simple and cheap(er), but
  the more comfortable and more efficient electrical models are
  making inroads with compact measurements, quiet operation
  and low energy and water use. Electric heads are easier to
  work for non-sailors, and might clog a little less often, because they have macerator evacuation pumps that grind up
  waste and toilet paper before anything goes into the holding
  tank. "Raritan's Lectrasan heads and Groco's Thermopure are
  ahead of the EPA regulations if killing coliform bacteria is
  what you want to do," said West Marine's Chuck Hawley.
  "These systems do not use chlorine but heat. They are MSD
  1 devices by Coast Guard standards and can be installed on
  uninspected vessels up to 65 feet in length. They do not,
  however, address the nutrient and oxygen issues that are associated with sewage discharge."

More useful head advice can be found in the West Advisor section on the West Marine Web site.

A greener solution

The head game would not be complete without bringing up the greenest of all toilets, the composting head. I remember a conversation with one sailing magazine publisher who expressed disgust about boat toilets that use a natural composting process instead of a conventional plumbing system that separates us from our waste at once. Flushing and forgetting is all we know, but there are downsides to it, besides the exorbitant water use. Water toilets are tied to increasingly antiquated sewer systems that are undersized and in dire need of repair. But the upgrades are extensive and expensive and municipalities are pressed for cash, so they are on the waiting list. In late February of 2009 things came to a head (pardon the pun) when rain caused a sewage spill of approximately 900,000 gallons in Richmond, California, contaminating San Francisco Bay and forcing the cancellation of the popular small-boat weekend at Richmond Yacht Club. For years similar spills have happened in many crowded metro areas in the U.S.

Composting toilets are simple, compact and effective in conserving water, because they don't have to be flushed. That means they don't need complex plumbing either, which is the part that makes boat heads such an unappetizing proposition in case of failure. Air Head, a manufacturer of such systems claims up to one season's worth of use for weekend sailors (80 uses) or 60 uses for a liveaboard couple before the composting bin has to be emptied. The drawback of composting toilets is that they take their time and require some user involvement.

Composting heads are well-ventilated containers that provide the environment for aerobic bacteria to break down organic matter and transform it into humus. The key difference to water toilets is the separation of liquid and solid waste, either by draining or evaporation, which is necessary for a proper decomposing process. Bulking agents such as grass clippings, leaves, sawdust, or finely chopped straw can be added to help aeration and provide nutrients for microbial growth. To keep decomposition going, periodic turning and removal of the compost is required. That's part of the deal and distinctly different from the flush-and-forget system. Will it work for you? It depends on your style of sailing and the commitment to the cause.

Pros:

- Decomposition is a natural process
- Conserves water
- Less pressure on the environment
- Simple, compact
- No plumbing
- No messy pump-outs (but the urine container has to be emptied)
- No schlepping of holding tanks
- No or low power consumption
- Compost is good for the garden

Cons:

- Maintaining system requires user commitment and involvement
- Neglect will disrupt composting process and can cause health consequences
- Removal of incompletely decomposed solids is worse than emptying holding tank
- Still might need septic system to treat other forms of waste
- Comfort units require power

What about showers? Water from the galley sink and the shower is commonly known as gray water. It contains soap and chemicals such as phosphates and nitrates that can potentially lead to nutrient enrichment and algal blooms if dumped in large quantities. Algal blooms reduce light penetration, which further reduces dissolved oxygen levels, which makes beaches inhospitable to swimmers and whole bodies of water unappetizing to sail on. Compared to the quantities dumped by municipal wastewater treatment plants and agriculture, the contribution from boats is small, but not small enough to be ignored. At the very least, consider using alternative cleaners that are biodegradable and contain fewer or no chemicals at all. Avoid products that contain phosphates, E.D.T.A. (ethylenediamine-tetra-acetic acid), sodium tripolyphosphate

(STPP), enzymes, optical brighteners, chlorine bleaches, chemical plasticizers, formaldehyde, sodium tallowate, synthetic dyes and perfumes, tricolsan and titanium dioxide.

SOURCES:
Boatbookings.com: www.boatbookings.com
BoatU.S. Foundation: www.boatus.com/foundation/cleanwater/
    sewage.asp
Ecker Yachting: www.eckeryachting.com
The Green Blue: www.thegreenblue.org.uk
TUI Marine: www.tuimarine.com
Marine Sanitation Devices
Groco: www.groco.net
Raritan: www.raritaneng.com
West Marine: www.westmarine.com
Composting toilets:
Air Head: www.airheadtoilet.com
Eco John: www.ecojohn.com
Nature's Head: www.natureshead.net
Toilet in a bag:
Philips Environmental Research: www.thepett.com

Maintaining the Edge

Pride of ownership demands a shipshape vessel, which requires a certain dedication to maintenance chores. However, boat maintenance also is good business with solid profit margins and a bewildering choice of products. Even the condensed version of West Marine's catalog still has 50 pages of paints, lubes, adhesives, sealants, putties, fillers, soaps, cleaners, polishes, waxes and protectants, plus tools and accessories. Each boater has different needs and preferences so there is a lot of variety. But thinking beyond personal needs, the underlying question becomes: How good and how necessary are those products and what's their ecological impact? Lubrication and boat care products tend to get into the environment almost immediately and with them harmful contents such as chlorine, ammonia, potassium hydroxide and solvents, which are no friends of aquatic flora or fauna. Detergents contain phosphates that cause local oxygen depletion, which can suffocate aquatic life and many chemical formulations have the potential to disrupt the reproductive cycle of fish. So a little greening of maintenance products seems in order. But how does that work without making them ineffective?

Clean and green

There is no shortage of manufacturers' claims for the eco-friendliness of their products, but that is no guarantee. "Ten years ago we identified green and biodegradable products, but we never were comfortable with the claims and backing them up," conceded Chuck

Hawley, who oversees all product information at West Marine. "There was a lack of standards so we were in danger of over-promising and not delivering." The labels or logos of such products often depict marine life and use positive adjectives such as "friendly," "safe," "organic" or "pure." At the very least, label or packaging use a variation of the color green. "Greenwashing," as the unfounded claims of environmental benefits are often called, has been rampant across many industries, not just boating. It tarnished the principle of sustainability and hurt companies that made an honest effort. Therefore, a universally recognized and verifiable certification was badly needed.

Internationally, there is the ISO 14021 standard for environmental claims that assures that the information about the impact of consumer products is specific, accurate, clear, relevant, and in line with common definitions. The use of terms such as biodegradable, compostable, recyclable or reduced energy consumption is subject to detailed guidance. Consumers also must be given opportunity to inquire, comment and complain should they feel so inclined. West Marine joined the EPA's Design for the Environment program, and has introduced its own brand of boat care products that are certified to be safer for humans and the environment. Products are tested by the EPA and receive the DfE logo if they are compliant with the regulations. They have to be made from approved chemicals and ingredients, they have to be packaged lightly with recycled or recyclable materials, they can't undergo animal testing, and their benefit claims must be verifiable. But they also need to perform as well as or better than conventional products and they have to be competitively priced to represent a true alternative.

The number of DfE-certified products is increasing fast and the EPA claims that thus far the program has helped eliminate 270 million pounds of environmentally dangerous chemicals. "We are not chemists or environmental scientists," Hawley said, "but now we are looking for vendors who comply to those standards and whose products have earned the DfE logo." In 2008 West Marine decided that beginning in 2015 it will only carry certified maintenance products with best-in-class ingredients and minimum environmental impact. The process will take time because the devil is in the details, as Hawley pointed out: "Now there are lubricants that are based on canola oil, which biodegrade to 90 percent in 28 days and to 100 percent in 42 days. But it is tricky. If you have a bilge cleaner that biode-grades, but does not dissolve oil and grease, the whole product does not make sense."

BoatU.S. suggests alternatives for boaters who want to make sure they know all the ingredients of their cleaning agents, which means mixing the cocktails themselves. Customers are advised to scrutinize the label before buying and stick with products that are non-toxic, phosphate- and chlorine-free. Phosphates act as a fertil-izer promoting algal growth, and chlorine has no place in the ma-rine environment. It's best to use cleaners sparingly but with a lot of elbow grease, and toss toxic products into the appropriate waste bin at the marina, or dispose of them with the HAZMAT recycling sta-tion. Whenever possible, they should be used on the hard, since spilling them into the water, i.e. by rinsing them off, would consti-tute a violation of the Clean Water Act.

Following are some ideas for cheaper, gentler and more sensible potions to keep your vessel shipshape. There are a handful of house-hold staples that can be used for almost all cleaning jobs when mixed with each other in different concentrations. If your galley has baking soda, vinegar, vegetable oil-based soap, hydrogen peroxide, sodium carbonate, and essential oils for scenting, you're in business. One word of caution from the cleaning experts: Before applying self-formulated solutions on large areas, they suggest trying them on a test surface.

- Surface cleaner: Vinegar and water cleans most surfaces.
- All-purpose cleaner: Two tablespoons of vinegar, one tea-spoon of washing soda, two cups of hot water and ¼ cup of liquid soap. Mix all ingredients, but soap. Put in a spray bot-tle and add soap. Mix gently, apply, wipe clean.
- Scouring paste: Mix ⅔ cup of baking soda with ½ cup of liq-uid soap and a little bit of water to make a paste and stir in two tablespoons of vinegar.
- Drain cleaner: Pour ½ cup of baking soda down the drain, fol-lowed by ½ cup of vinegar. Plug drain and let sit for 15 min-utes. Pour two quarts of boiling water. Regular use helps prevent clogs. Opening clogs can also be done with com-pressed air or, if all else fails, by a mechanical snake.
- Fiberglass stains: Make a paste of baking soda and water, but

be gentle since baking soda is an abrasive. Rinse with lemon or lime juice.

- Chrome: Apple cider vinegar and a soft cloth, then use a dab of baby oil to restore the shine. Club soda also works as polish.
- Windows and mirrors: Mix one cup vinegar, with one quart water, put in a spray bottle, rinse and squeegee. Add a tablespoon of lemon juice for scent.
- Brass: Worchester sauce, or a paste made of equal amounts of vinegar, salt and water.
- Copper fittings: Use a solution of lemon juice and water.
- Decks: Use a mixture of one part white vinegar to eight parts warm water.
- Stainless steel: Clean with a cloth and undiluted white vinegar.
- Aluminum: Clean with a solution of two tablespoons cream of tartar and one quart of hot water on a soft cloth.
- Teak: Use mild powder soap and bronze wool.
- Interior Woods: Clean with olive or almond oil, but only use on interior woods because they won't hold up in direct sunlight.
- Plastic: Mix vinegar and water 1:2.

SOURCES:
BoatU.S.: www.boatus.com/foundation/cleanwater/drops/
    Preventive.asp
Design for the Environment: www.epa.gov/dfe
The Green Blue: www.thegreenblue.org.uk/greendirectory/
    documents/GreenClaims.pdf
West Marine: www.westmarine.com
Oregon Metro: www.oregonmetro.gov/index.cfm/go/by.web/
    id=1400

The copper conundrum

There is little dispute about the fact that clean bottoms are fast bottoms. But keeping them clean is the quintessential fight for sailors who have their boats in the water most of the year. Vessels that sit unused for days or weeks on end are prime targets for the invasion of microorganisms that settle on the underwater portion of the hull and the appendages. This process is known as fouling and varies drastically by sailing venue. Its extent depends on factors like tem-

Photo 10.1 Proper protection for workers and environment no longer is a luxury, but a requirement. Here a yard worker cleans a hull bottom with Soda Blast, an environmentally friendly method for removing old paint (www.soda blastsystems.com). *SodaBlast Systems*

perature, salinity, and nutrients contained in the water. But the headaches caused by an overgrown bottom are the same: Impaired boat speed and maneuverability and higher fuel bills. Not to mention the ruined aesthetics that are on full display when sailing to weather with a good degree of heel. The common remedy to the malady is drysailing, which means storing the boat on a trailer when it's not in use. If that isn't an option, the only recourse is regular renewal of the antifouling bottom paint, which is one of the messiest, most dreaded and costly maintenance expenditures for sailboat owners. And it's those antifouling paints that are coming under increased scrutiny. They contain copper and other biocides that retard marine growth on the hull and are leached into the water in "controlled fashion." Copper has been used as antifouling for hundreds of years and the paint industry likes to point out it's much less harmful to marine organisms than the effective but toxic tributyltin (TBT), which now is banned in most places. This ban resulted in a shift back to copper as the main biocide, which is included in antifouling paints as cuprous oxide, cuprous thiocyanate and metallic copper powder. These paint products work on most hull materials, except on aluminum, where copper causes galvanic corrosion.

Although the performance of copper-based biocides is less powerful than TBT, they will be in use for the foreseeable future with "booster biocides" added for better efficacy. Copper pollution in the water doesn't come from pleasure boats alone. Not even the large ocean-going ships are the chief culprit, because it is mostly caused by shoreside polluters such as industrial wastewater, atmospheric debris, i.e. from foundries and metal plating and cleaning operations, but also by fungicides, or wood preservatives.

How bad is copper? It is on the table of elements and occurs naturally in the environment. It is part of humans, at least in low concentrations. Industrial products that contain copper are used in crop dusting, vitamins, water pipes, roof shingles, wiring, and computers. The Green Blue takes a cautious approach, stating that "due to its complex nature and the uncertainty over its level of interaction with other substances, it is difficult to establish the precise effect of elevated levels of copper in the marine environment." Citing a 1984 study, the organization said that there is evidence for certain species of fish and other marine organisms to be sensitive to low levels of copper.

In 1996, the Shelter Island Yacht Basin in San Diego, California, a large yacht harbor with hundreds of recreational vessels that are docked at various clubs and marinas, was put on the list of impaired waters due to elevated levels of dissolved copper in the water column. The Clean Water Act required the regional board to establish a Total Maximum Daily Load for copper. According to Resolution No. R9-2005-0019, the goal is keeping the concentration in seawater at or below 3.1 micrograms per liter (approximately one quart) for continuous exposure and 4.8 micrograms per liter for peak exposure. The San Diego Unified Port District has been overseeing a study that examines various antifouling coatings and their effectiveness. The first phase of the project tested 200 different kinds of antifouling paint on fiberglass panels, placed underwater at marinas and yacht clubs along San Diego's Shelter Island. The second phase included testing of coatings on boat hulls. The port was in line to receive $190,000 in funding for the project through an EPA Pollution Prevention Grant, and said it was matching that amount.

"This [project] has to be taken in context, because there seem to be many sailboats with hard antifouling paint with up to 70 percent of copper content," commented Bob Donat, vice president of paint manufacturer Interlux. "Divers then clean these boat bottoms regularly and there is little water flush and tidal exchange, which contributes to the problem." The battle here is not about banning copper outright, but reducing it and combining it with other biocides. Donat also pointed out the importance of paint formulation, which dictates how much and how quickly copper is released into the environment. It has to do with the resin system in the paint that functions like a cold capsule, releasing medication little by little over a certain period of time.

Copper as a biocide isn't done yet, but it is getting competition from antifouling paints that use less or none of it: Composite of copper and silica sand, for instance, produce a lighter paint with 40 percent less copper content. Another alternative is white copper that is lighter than cuprous oxide and effective in lower concentration. It also makes it possible to mix brighter colors. The killer application for biocides however, at least in some experts' opinion, could be Econea, a metal-free antifouling agent that protects boat hulls without accumulating in the marine environment, according to manufacturer Janssen Preservation & Material Protection. "Compared to metal-based antifouling products, Econea provides exceptional antifouling protection at low usage levels," the company Web site explained. "It's more effective than copper-based paints containing cuprous thiocyanate, and just as effective as those containing cuprous oxide. Econea degrades rapidly and its degradation products are biodegradable. As a result, it is a better option for the marine environment." Pettit Paint of Rockaway, New Jersey, touts zinc omadine as an extremely effective biocide against marine slime, algae and other soft growth. It's safe enough so "the FDA approves its use in anti-dandruff shampoos," the company said in a statement.

Another issue of paint application is the emission of volatile organic compounds (VOC), which contribute to ozone formation and are harmful for humans when inhaled. ePaint, based in Massachusetts, has introduced Ecominder, a series of water-based bottom paint products that are zero-VOC and copper free. Instead, the company says, they contain "novel photoactive technology with environmentally preferred active ingredients to provide [customers] with a safe, effective alternative to traditional bottom paints." Photo-active pigments when exposed to sunlight produce hydrogen perox-ide, which in turn creates a protective barrier. Another advantage of non-toxic, water-based paints is the flexibility of application, because they can go on at low temperatures.

But low temperatures are of little concern in San Diego, which has become Ground Zero for the development of new bottom paint formulations. Given that it took 20 years for TBT to get banned ef-fectively in industrialized countries (it still can be found in the de-veloping world), changes shouldn't be expected to happen overnight. But once the new low-impact paints are proven to be competitive in pricing and performance, copper too might become a memory.

Hull cleaning

No matter what kind of race is on the calendar, winning or finish-ing well is a matter of a well-prepared boat and that includes an im-peccably clean bottom. And that requires a good deal of money to pay for a trusted diver who usually is in high demand by everyone in the marina. Regatta sailors know the routine. When preparing his Cal 40, ILLUSION, for a Transpacific Yacht Race in 2003, famed U.S. offshore racer Stan Honey made sure the diver was coming out the morning of the start to clean the boat's burnished underwater paint for maximum effect. And what's good for racing is also good for weekend sailing, so underwater hull cleaners are also called upon by average sailing folks who keep their boats in the water and consider clean bottoms part of routine maintenance. This job boosts the boat's performance and the fun of sailing it while lowering operation costs. Done right, and *right* is the operative word, it can also help the marine environment by reducing pollution and extend the life of hull paints. Funded by NOAA, the National Sea Grant College Program, the Department of Commerce, the California Sea Grant Program, the EPA, the California State Resources Agency among others, the University of California at Davis published some sugges-tions titled "Underwater Hull Cleaner's Best Management Prac-tices." It starts with preventing copper paints from entering the water and sediments. Divers are advised to keep the antifouling paint intact and remove only actual growth to reduce drag and fuel use. A few worthy thoughts before reaching for a sandblaster, a paintbrush, or calling the diver:

- Regular and gentle hull cleaning reduces marine growth and hull drag.
- Wait 90 days after applying new paint before hiring a diver. Paints release more toxicant when new.
- Soft sloughing or ablative paints release toxicants when cleaned. On these boats, clean only running gear and zinc anodes.
- Insist on sponges or other soft materials as cleaning tools.
- Stainless-steel brushes or scrubbing pads should only be applied to unpainted metal surfaces.
- Don't sand or strip hull paint under water.
- Bring zinc anodes back to shore; recycle or dispose properly.
- Clean gently to avoid creating a plume or cloud of paint in the water.
- Consider alternative hull paints, or low VOC, copper free and/or water-based paints that can be scrubbed by a diver without harming the environment.
- Correct application extends paint life.
- Consult with experts before you put on new type of paint. Make sure it works for your style of sailing, understand the prep requirements, and calculate the necessary quantity.
- Repair paint bonding problems at haul out to avoid further chipping and flaking of paint into the water.
- Antifouling paints, primers, solvents and all painting tools have to be disposed off properly at the marina or brought to a HAZMAT facility.
- Refrain from underwater cleaning of sloughing and ablative (self polishing) hull paints since they release copper. Antifouling paints with hard finishes release less toxins during underwater cleaning.
- Polyurethane and silicone paints won't rub off during underwater cleaning and don't contain a lot of toxins, but they are not as effective in growth retardation.
- Consider drysailing or put the boat on a floating hoist (if possible) if you want to cut back on pesky bottom maintenance. It's relief for the environment and your checkbook.

So aside from painting and scrubbing, there are solutions to the copper conundrum, but they come at a price: Eco-friendly and copper-less paint can run up to $270 per gallon, which is a lot of green for green paint, especially if a boat has a large underwater surface area, and needs two coats. But there is a cheaper solution to the problem, too: Sail more, so the boat doesn't grow a beard and the diver doesn't have to scrape the bottom as often.

SOURCES:
Clean Water Act: http://www.epa.gov/lawsregs/laws/cwa.html
The Green Blue: www.thegreenblue.org.uk
Interlux: www.yachtpaint.com
Pettit Paint: www.pettitpaint.com
ePaint: www.epaint.com
San Diego Unified Port District Safer Alternatives to Copper
    Antifouling Paints Project: www.portofsandiego.org/
    environment/alternative-hull-paints.html
University of California Hull Cleaners BMP:
    http://seagrant.ucdavis.edu/hullclean.htm
West Marine: www.westmarine.com

Clean marinas

Boats require work. It's called routine maintenance and it's a ritual that occurs every spring when boats are woken up from hibernation and in the fall, when they're being put back to bed. Not all jobs are created equal, just as some owners are do-it-yourselfers while others are checkbook boaters who outsource every task. And even during a down cycle in the economy, few marina yards complain about zero business. Part of this development can be attributed to the boats' complicated and service-hungry systems that are being installed to boost convenience and comfort—and to generate additional revenue for builders and suppliers. Much of this sophisticated gear is complicated to service and maintain, so trained experts are required.

All this doesn't mean that the messy jobs have gone away. However, now that their impact on the environment is better understood, the rules for working on boat jobs have changed. Gone are the days where owners were free to do whatever they wanted and however they saw fit when they doctored around on their boats out in the lot, off to the side, behind the brambles. "Pollutants from marinas can result in toxicity in the water column, both lethal and sublethal, related to decreased levels of dissolved oxygen and elevated levels of metals and petroleum hydrocarbons," the EPA states in the agency's Guidance Specifying Management Measures for Sources of Nonpoint Pollution in Coastal Waters. "These pollutants may enter the water through discharges from boats or other sources, spills, or storm water runoff." Hence smart marina and boatyard businesses have been cleaning up their act, because they are legally required to do it and because common sense suggests that clean business is good business. Actually, it's the only business that is going to be around in the future.

With increasing environmental awareness and more stringent regulations, boat maintenance is evolving in many different aspects, but not all of them are necessarily high-tech. "We have to use biodegradable and much less aggressive cleaners, solvents and polishes," said Keith Mayes, who managed the detailing department at the Hinckley Yard in Portsmouth, Rhode Island. "Once the yard is done, we get our turn with soap, shammy and polish. After we finish, a 10 year-old boat has to look like new, which is what our customers expect. But nowadays this job requires more elbow grease, which translates into more time spent on each boat." Mayes estimated that a first-rate detailing job would take about 25 man-hours.

"We have to manage different waste streams, from storm run-off to lead dust and proper disposal of chemicals, oil and gasoline," explained Rives Potts, who manages the Brewer Yacht Yard at Pilots Point Marina, Essex, Connecticut. "It all used to go into the dumpster. Now we have 17 or 18 different barrels that all have to be properly disposed off. You have to train the workers where to put which rag and the haulers need to be credible. It takes a consistent effort all around." And it takes money. Infrastructure improvements are included in the yard bills, which seem to be going up by a few percent every year. Some places charge an environmental fee as a separate line item on each bill instead of hiding it in the labor costs, so customers can easily identify it.

Yards also are investing in clean technologies such as Festools for dust-free sanding, paint booths with sophisticated filtration and proper waste management. Compliance with environmental regulations might have been trendy once, but now it is part of doing business. Scrubbing bottoms with the boat in the water is becoming restricted or downright illegal in many places, just like it has been in some European countries. It's the most common of all boat chores and all yards and marinas have to deal with it. But many are standing pat to learn about wash-down guidelines that are being developed by the states and/or the EPA before they invest in new systems or upgrade existing ones.

Educational literature published by the Green Blue discusses three sophisticated closed-loop wash-down systems that include treatment and recycling.

- Flocculation uses a special agent that's added to the run-off water to get particles to aggregate into clumps that sink to the bottom of the catchment tank before they can be collected and disposed properly. The resulting water can then be recirculated for wash down.
- Ozone treatment incorporates an ozone generator for the decontamination process. Ozone bubbles percolate through the catchment tank to oxidize the dissolved pollutants and eliminate offensive odors, without the use of toxic chemicals.
- Cyclonic filtration uses rotation and vortex separation to remove up to 98 percent of solid waste particles in the first pass while discharging them into a separate container. The centrifugal force that's generated during cyclonic filtration is especially effective in filtering heavier contaminants such as lead and copper.

A point of contention is the legal requirements that can differ for work done by the yard and by the boat owner, even if the jobs are the same. Logic suggests that the rules that apply to the yard also should apply to DIYers. But that's not necessarily how it works. "Boats are classified as households and therefore the owners could dump everything into the household waste," Potts said. "That doesn't make sense." Brewers, Potts said, tries to hold owners to the same standards as the yard crews and installed recycling centers. "It's got to be convenient, otherwise it is hard to follow."

The ticket to clean boat yards in the U.S. is the so-called Clean Marina Initiative, a voluntary, incentive-based program promoted by NOAA and others to encourage marina operators and boaters alike to protect water quality with environmentally sound operating and maintenance procedures. There are two catalysts for this initiative: One is the growth of recreational boating during the 1990s, which increased by 14 percent according to a Coast Guard report. From that followed that pollution from boating activities and from marinas also increased. "Pollutants created by marina activities are released directly into the water," NOAA stated in the Clean Marina brief. "Although not one of the leading sources of polluted runoff, pollution from marinas can have a significant impact on local water quality. Therefore, it is important to promote operation and maintenance practices that will prevent pollution from entering coastal waterways."

The second is the Coastal Zone Act Reauthorization Amendment of 1990 that requires coastal states (including Great Lakes states) with approved coastal zone management programs to address runoff pollution with measures that are approved by the EPA and NOAA, the two agencies that administer the Coastal Nonpoint Pollution Control Program. EPA guidelines talk about "economically achievable measures that reflect the best available technology for reducing pollutants," but leave the states freedom to choose from a wide range of practices, which run the gamut: Marina flushing, water quality and habitat assessment, shoreline stabilization, stormwater runoff, fuel dock design, sewage facilities, solid and fish waste disposal, liquid materials (i.e. cleaning fluids), petroleum control, boat cleaning, sewage facility maintenance, public education, and prevention of ecological problems that are being caused by inconsiderate or reckless boat operation in sensitive shallow-water habitat areas.

BoatU.S. also promotes the Clean Marina Initiative. "We facilitate information exchange," Susan Shingledecker of the BoatU.S. Foundation said. "However the program is desperately underfunded and does not exist in inland states, since it is linked to NOAA's coastal management program." Still, BoatU.S. encourages boaters to consider patronizing certified Clean Marinas that have voluntarily adopted environmentally friendly practices, espousing "clean, well-lit bathrooms, shoreside laundry facilities, more grassy areas, convenient pump-out stations, plenty of trash cans and recycling bins, and many other amenities that not only help keep the waterway clean but make your time at the marina more pleasant."

NOAA meanwhile points to the economic advantages, such as reducing waste and the cost of disposal or attracting more business from eco-conscious boaters who support cleaner and greener marina facilities. Keeping track of what goes in the water and how it affects the environment impacts the yard business profoundly. "Sediment testing used to occur once every 10 years and cost $800-900," Potts said. "Now it occurs every three years and costs $50,000. That's because they have a bigger microscope now and are looking for more trace elements, some of which don't originate from a boatyard, such as cadmium."

The real cost of running a clean operation are stunning compared to the dirty old days of dumping, but yard operators recognize the need to invest to stay in business. How well does this sit with customers? Potts and other marina managers insist that the vast majority of boaters are in favor of environmental responsibility, as long as they know what to do and it does not inconvenience them. "Walking into the bathroom splattered in paint used to be a badge of honor. Now we know that it can kill you," Potts said.

Some examples for best yard practices:

- When power washing on the travel lift or the hoist, prevent loose antifouling paint flakes from entering the water, i.e. with a loop of rope that traps paint particles that can be swept up and disposed off properly.
- Skirt the hull when scrubbing down or re-painting the bottom and use a tarp to catch old paint flakes and fresh drips.
- Make sure you know where to dispose the paint chips.
- If you have to sand, use a dustless vacuum sander (or connect the existing sander to a ShopVac) to keep toxic dust from flying around and use proper protective gear (respirator and suit) to protect your health. If you don't have dustless sanding equipment, ask if you can rent it from the yard.
- Don't spill. Make sure there's a tarp under the keel so you won't leave a paint spot when you're done.
- Avoid sanding and painting when the boat is in the water.
- Use "soft" cleaners whenever possible.
- Clean and store the tools when the job is finished or you are leaving for the day, and keep paint receptacles covered.
- If it hasn't happened already, ask marina management to set

up recycling bins not just for glass, paper and plastics, but also for the hazardous materials like paints, solvents, epoxies and soiled tools.

◆ If you can, select a marina or yard that participates in the Clean Marina Initiative and adheres to best practices.

SOURCES:

BoatU.S.: www.boatus.com/foundation/cleanwater/marinas.asp

Clean Marina case studies: http://www.epa.gov/owow/nps/ marinas/index.html

The Green Blue: www.thegreenblue.org.uk/publications/index.asp

NOAA Ocean and Coastal Resource Management: www.coastalmanagement.noaa.gov/marinas.html

11

The Plight of Plastic

"I just want to say one word to you—just one word—plastics. Think about it. There's a great future in plastics." Mr. McGuire's advice to Benjamin Braddock in the movie *The Graduate* was a line for the ages. Starring a baby-faced Dustin Hoffman and Anne Bancroft, this acclaimed satirical comedy told the story of a young man's seduction by an older woman, and how this experience shaped his life. The year was 1967 and it remains etched in history as the Summer of Love with hippies, free love, civil rights, anti-war protests and political dissent. And plastic had become one of the symbols of the generation gap. To the establishment, it symbolized progress and a brighter future, but to the counterculture it was synonymous for greed, materialism and superficiality.

Right around that time, the marine industry was experiencing the plastic revolution. Everybody seemed to build fiberglass boats or buy them, because they were cheap, easy to make, and durable to boot.

For boating, and for countless other industries, plastic indeed was a godsend and it's become so pervasive that it's hard to imagine what life would be like without it.

But too much of a good thing isn't necessarily wonderful. It could be unsustainable, too. Plastic products, including fiberglass boats, are made from nonrenewable resources like fossil fuels. It's a process that takes a lot of energy and water and produces plenty of carbon emissions. Plastic also proliferates and accumulates. Like spam mail, it keeps coming and coming. But unlike spam that can be deleted, conventional plastic has an impressive half-life since it doesn't rot or biodegrade. The Consumer Reports' Greener Choices Web site quoted production data by the American Chemistry Council, saying that a total of about 116 billion pounds of plastic was manufactured in the U.S. in 2007. The EPA said that the amount of plastic in municipal solid waste has increased from less than one percent in 1960 to about 12 percent in 2006 while the recycling rate of the popular polyethylene terephthalate (PET) containers declined. These are everybody's favorite water or soda bottles that get used once before they get tossed in the trash or, to a much smaller extent, into a recycling bin. They are made of thermoplastic polymer resin, a member of the polyester family, which surfaces in thousands of different applications, from textiles to boats. The Container Recycling Institute estimated that in 1995, one in four PET containers were recycled, but in 2006, less than one in five. This means that of the 72 billion PET plastic beverage bottles purchased in 2006, about 50 billion ended up as litter, perhaps in an incinerator, but more likely as landfill or, worse, as "oceanfill."

"Suddenly the plastic water bottle—long seen as a cool accessory carried by sports teams and thirsty people on the go—is being seen as antisocial," a story in the United Nations Environment Program TUNZA magazine said. "The approximately 200 billion liters (53 billion gallons) of bottled water consumed each year is increasingly being recognized as a massive waste of resources in a world where they are getting ever scarcer. Enough oil to fuel 100,000 cars is used just to make a year's worth of plastic water bottles in North America alone. And more fossil fuels are burned—helping to warm the planet—in shipping the water around the world. . . . For every liter of water poured into a bottle, another two are used in its manufacture." It's time to get off the bottle. *Those* bottles, at least.

The Project AWARE Foundation, a global nonprofit organization of scuba divers and water enthusiasts that traffics in ocean conservation, estimates that nearly 90 percent of all marine debris is made of some form of plastic which outweighs zooplankton at least by a factor of 6:1. Estimates put the average personal plastic use at about 200 pounds per year, but that number is expected to climb to 300. Approximately100 billion plastic shopping bags are being used annually in the U.S., which makes me wonder how people got their groceries home in the pre-plastic era.

Plastic is all around us, because it is extremely convenient: Use it once and toss it. But then what? We can throw it out, but we can't throw it away. If recycling really worked as we are led to believe, there wouldn't be a Texas-sized stretch of ocean, known as the Great Pacific Garbage Patch (actually, there are multiple parts to it) lazily rotating and sucking up all the plastic debris that floats along on the ocean currents from all points of the compass. From the surface down to a depth of several hundred feet, the water column carries millions of tons of plastic trash: Bottles, caps, lighters, asthma inhalers, fishing gear, tennis shoes, flip-flops, rubber duckies, Legos, condoms, anything and everything we use can be found in the GPGP where it ends up after starting its journey on land via the waterways in highly populated metro areas. When thrown out, plastic merely disappears from the consumer's sight, but it won't go away. It has a future, but not the one Mr. McGuire in *The Graduate* might have had in mind.

"Recycling rates are horrible," said Markus Eriksen, director of research and education at the Algalita Foundation, a nonprofit ded-

Photo 11.1 JUNK RAFT might not be the prettiest yacht to cross an ocean, but she's one of the few built entirely from recycled stuff. During the 2,200 mile voyage from Los Angeles to Hawaii JUNK RAFT raised awareness for the plastic problem that plagues the Pacific Ocean. *Junk Raft*

icated to researching the effects of trash in the ocean. "We have to stop making disposable plastics that are not biodegradable. It doesn't make sense to wrap food for a few days with material that then stays in the landfill or in the ocean for hundreds of years." Eriksen was one of the crew on JUNK RAFT, a raft made from 15,000 recycled bottles that were tied together with a fishing net. About 13,000 were soda bottles while 2,000 were donated Nalgene bottles. On top of this was a deck that consisted of 30 old sailboat masts and on top of that a fuselage of a Cessna 310 aircraft. The rig was an A-frame that consisted of two old sailboat masts.

It wasn't pretty but it was made of recycled stuff, save for the electronics. It took JUNK RAFT 87 days to sail the 2,225 miles from Long Beach, California, to Honolulu, Hawaii, which is not much shorter than it would take a piece of trash to drift the same distance with favorable winds and currents. "All abandoned boats from California drift out to sea and end up in Hawaii," joked Eriksen's crewmate Joel Paschal, an ocean scientist. The goal of this journey was to attract attention to plastic in the marine environment. Correcting this problem will take time and a miracle, because trash is dumped into the ocean at an alarming rate. "Over the last 10 years alone the amount of trash in the oceans has doubled," Eriksen pointed out. "Recycling is not a solution. You can only re-use plastic to make some lower-grade plastics. You can't make a food-grade container from a container you commit to recycling. The FDA won't approve it. Most of our plastic trash goes to China where it gets down-cycled into cheap products." Added Paschal: "A feasible cleanup starts at the source. Stop utilizing one-time-use plastics, so they won't get into the ocean, then worry about collecting it."

But there are more alarming facts. The plastic that's already in the sea breaks down into smaller and smaller pieces that are being ingested by birds, fish and mammals, so it gets introduced into the food chain, and very likely to the human dinner table. "Plastic is not harmlessly drifting around, but it absorbs and releases toxins, Eriksen noted. "It releases chemical additives and plasticizers into the ocean. Plastic also absorbs hydrophobic pollutants, like Polychlorinated biphenyls (PCBs), and pesticides like DDT. (While DDT is a known environmental bomb and has been banned in the U.S., PCB is a little more obscure, but it affects us, nonetheless. In 1976, for instance, the New York State Department of Environmental Conser-

Photo 11.2 Plastic trash in the ocean does not break down, it only breaks up. This bottle was picked up by the JUNK RAFT crew. The missing pieces are still floating in the ocean or have been ingested by marine life. *Junk Raft*

vation banned fishing in the Hudson River because the high PCB levels in fish posed health risks to humans.) These pollutants bio-accumulate in the tissues of marine organisms, bio-magnify up the food chain, and find their way into the foods we eat." According to Eriksen, one third of the fish he and Paschal caught on this trip had shards of plastic in them.

A little past the half-way point, U.K. ocean rower celebrity Roz Savage tied up to JUNK RAFT. She too was en route to Hawaii from California, but had run into trouble with her watermaker. It was a chance for Eriksen and Paschal to spread their gospel. Aside from swapping gear for food, Savage also included a plea for the reduction of plastic use on her Web site. In the spring of 2009, Eriksen embarked on a sequel to JUNK RAFT by pedaling down the West

Photo 11.3 Garbage on this beach in Micronesia is mostly plastic that had drifted in on the tide. *Wolf Slanec*

Coast on a bicycle for an educational trip called *Junk Ride*. That expedition led from Vancouver, British Columbia to Tijuana, Mexico, and made many stops to share samples of plastic trash from the ocean with schools, companies, and political leaders and to deliver the message that yes, there's a future for plastics, but one that comes fraught with problems for environment and people.

From Plastic to PLASTIKI

"I think that the most important thing is not to make plastic the enemy, but to really reassess how we use, dispose, and reuse it," said David de Rothschild, adventurer, environmentalist and heir to the Rothschild banking empire. "It comes down to the old cliché of stopping to think before you buy. Can you reuse the bottle that contained the water or soda you drank earlier? The small things can make a big difference. We can all minimize our impact if we fundamentally change the way in which we consume." Rothschild also battles plastic, but with a different tactic—and a boat that resembles a boat. His nonprofit *Adventure Ecology* is the umbrella for the PLASTIKI expedition, which planned to use a 60-foot catamaran that was designed to be fully recyclable after use. It consisted of rigid plastic stringers that held the shape and 12,000 recycled and pressurized water bottles for flotation. Unlike the low-budget JUNK RAFT, PLASTIKI had corporate sponsors and hoped to showcase engineering solutions such as non-toxic glue that's made from cashews and sugar. No epoxy or other noxious substances were allowed to build the boat, de Rothschild said. Crew quarters were housed in a geodesic dome that featured a solar shower and a compost toilet, plus solar panels and wind and bicycle generators. PLASTIKI was ready to sail about 11,000 nautical miles from San Francisco, California, to Sydney, Australia, along with de Rothschild and a team of researchers and scientists that would rotate in and out at the various stopovers.

The expedition was inspired by KON-TIKI, Thor Heyerdahl's balsa raft that he sailed from South America to the Tuamotu Islands in 1947 to prove that this type of journey could have been and probably was done by ancient seafarers. While Heyerdahl's vessel was a true bio-cruiser made from natural materials, de Rothschild's expedition vehicle is fully synthetic, but also fully recyclable. PLASTIKI is an ambitious project, but technical challenges during construction forced repeated postponements of the voyage. Still, de Rothschild was undeterred in his fundamental views. "If it is cheaper, we continue our dirty ways, so we need to change the system," de Rothschild said. Plastic has to be part of that solution, he insisted, urging producers, sellers and consumers to see value in it, and to use it as a resource (i.e. as building material), exactly how PLASTIKI does. "Think of it this way: We are an upgrade culture. We upgrade everything, cars, computers, software, girlfriends. Why not the planet?" To demonstrate that, de Rothschild enlisted the help of Josina Heyerdahl, the granddaughter of Thor, who was going to be on the boat for part of the voyage. He also put great stock in the global SMART competition, which stands for Science, Marketing, Art and Design, Research and Technology. It solicits ideas and tangible solutions to beat waste and offers a financial grant to the winners in each category.

JUNK RAFT and PLASTIKI are but two examples that raise awareness for the plastic issue, which is easy to pinpoint but difficult to resolve, because floating trash knows no boundaries. Like climate change it is global. "Marine litter is an environmental, economic, human health and aesthetic problem," states the 2009 UNEP report

Photo 11.4 PLASTIKI is more sophisticated than JUNK RAFT, designed to sail from San Francisco, Calif., to Sydney, Australia with adventurer David de Rothschild on board. Plastiki used recycled plastic bottles, but also a lot of new gear. *Courtesy Adventure Ecology*

"Marine Litter A Global Challenge." The report criticizes poor practices of waste management, lack of infrastructure and enforcement, and the public's inadequate understanding of the consequences. Whether it is plastic bags or plastic bottles, cigarette lighters, sneakers or Styrofoam cups, this stuff has no business in the ocean. For the time being, cutting it off at the source holds the most promise to choke off the river of plastic flowing into the ocean. Until plastic becomes biodegradable, which it is starting to do, and provisions for its proper disposal are built into the value chain, the consumer is left holding the bag—or the bottle. "We need to go full cycle, and go back to targeting packaging—either minimizing it or getting rid of it entirely—where it is just not necessary," de Rothschild told National Geographic Adventure. "The biggest change we can make is to rethink our buying habits and create more demand for positive change."

Better alternatives exist or are being developed, although they come with an asterisk. Plastics can be engineered so they dissolve in seawater or become biodegradable. But it's not always easy. Eco-friendly food containers and flatware made from corn-based plastic include polylactide (PLA) that requires industrial composting or a different process for recycling. "It sounds great," Betty McLaughlin, the executive director of the non-profit Container Recycling Institute told USA Today. "It's renewable, biodegradable and all that kind of stuff. But the practical matter is that you still have to grow the corn to extract the sugar from. And how many pesticides do you need to put into the soil to grow the corn?" Here too, the lesson is that there is no free lunch, not even for the lunch container and his ubiquitous cousin, the water bottle.

Some plastic smarts:

- Reduce: Whenever possible, cut down on the amount of plastics you use in the first place. Reusable shopping bags, aluminum water bottles, and refillable containers can go a long way toward minimizing the amount of plastics that enter the waste stream. Plan ahead when you go sailing and see where you can cut out plastic in favor of organic materials and reusable items.
- Go bio: More and more grocery stores are offering compostable plastic cutlery and biodegradable containers and bags made from corn starch rather than polyethylene.
- Know your plastic: Plastic products are labeled with codes for the type of material they're made of. Look for the codes on the bottom of plastic containers. The most commonly recycled plastic types #1-PET and #2-HDPE. The higher the number, the smaller the chance of it getting recycled.

- ◆ Get good advice: Call your waste management service and ask what they recycle or visit www.earth911.com and type in your ZIP code.
- ◆ Hit up your grocery store: They ought to recycle plastic bags and containers. Check www.plasticbagrecycling.org.
- ◆ Use recycled plastic: If you absolutely have to, try to use products made with post-consumer recycled content, which are made with materials that have actually been used, rather than with manufacturing waste that never reached consumers.

SOURCES:
Algalita foundation: www.algalita.org
California Integrated Waste Management Board:
    www.ciwmb.ca.gov/BizWaste/FactSheets/BuyRecycled.htm
Consumer Reports Greener Choices: www.greenerchoices.org/
    products.cfm?product=plastic&pcat=homegarden
Live Science: www.livescience.com/technology/070327_seawater_
    plastic.html
The Plastiki: www.theplastiki.com
Project Aware www.projectaware.org
UNEP Marine Litter Report:
    www.unep.org/pdf/UNEP_Marine_Litter-A_Global_
    Challenge.pdf
USA Today: www.usatoday.com/money/industries/manufacturing/
    2008-12-25-biodegradable-plastic_N.htm

It lasts a lifetime (or two)

Roughly 17 million pleasure boats are in use in the U.S. and by estimate, more than two thirds are made from fiberglass, the material that L. Francis Herreshoff once derided as "frozen snot." While aesthetically unappealing, the material revolutionized boats and thousands of other products like hot tubs, kitchen sinks, cars, planes etc., because it was well suited for mass production. Unlike wood, it required very little maintenance while offering superior durability. The material is aptly named because it is made from extremely fine fibers of glass, which are woven into mats of roving or chopped strands. But to build anything, these mats have to be saturated with a plastic resin such as polyester, vinylester or epoxy before they are laid into a form. The result is a composite material that science knows as fiber-reinforced polymer (FRP) or glass-reinforced plastic (GRP), but boaters usually call fiberglass. Often builders use a core material like PVC or Divinycell foam that adds stiffness and results in a sandwich laminate of very good strength-to-weight ratio. Modern composites that are used in racing yachts use carbon fiber that's even lighter and stronger, but also more complex and expensive in production. But overall, composite construction appeals to boat manufacturers, because it allows them to build cost-effective, uniform, light, strong, and durable structures.

"The problem of new fiberglass boats are the old ones," stated yacht designer Eric Sponberg. "They take up storage, dock space and water access. It is very hard to expand marinas or add more dockage to existing ones. Yet most of the boats just sit there. To say nothing of the illegal dumping grounds. The writing is on the wall and part of it is recycling dead, old boats." The success of fiberglass boats is also their undoing, because they last decades, not just a few years like cars and computers. This means that the used-boat market is burgeoning with cheap and serviceable vessels, while manufacturers struggle to sell new boats. On the other hand, products that last long don't have to be replaced as often, which is sustainable, because it reduces the consumption of raw materials. What still has to be sorted out is a sustainable way to recycle fiberglass boats once they become so-called End of Live Boats. "There I was, observing the delivery bay at production builder Beneteau, enjoying the scene, as design royalties for our firm roll out the door," Farr Yacht Design's vice president, Russell Bowler, wrote in *Professional Boatbuilder* magazine. "Then a pang of environmental conscience whispered, 'Where is all this plastic going to end up?'" The answer is short and pragmatic. "Take it to the landfill and drive a bulldozer over it," said John McKnight, NMMA's director of environmental and safety compliance. "We worked hard to find a recycling system for boats. But I own a boat and if I have to get rid of it, I'll landfill it. There's nothing more cost effective. Landfill is just too cheap in the U.S. You have to balance out what provides the best benefits per dollar." McKnight, who represents the interests of the marine manufacturers vis-à-vis the government, is correct about present practices. It's also correct that landfilling fiberglass is relatively harmless and doesn't produce excessive greenhouse gas emissions. What is missing from the picture is a vision that turns discarded fiberglass into a resource when landfill becomes more expensive and millions of boats will be headed for a date with the chainsaw. In all fairness, boat building makes up approximately 10 percent of the fiberglass industry, but even so the marine industry should take initiative and drive the process of developing a fiberglass-recycling scheme that's ecologically and economically viable before it is told to do so by the government.

Perhaps a variation of the wildly successful cash-for-clunkers program that enticed car owners with a hefty cash premium to trade in their gas-guzzlers for newer and more efficient vehicles, could work for the boating industry, too. U.S. legislators followed a successful European example by passing H R 2751, the Consumer Assistance to Recycle and Save Act with a 298 to 119 margin in June of 2009. This bill was supposed to "accelerate motor fuel savings nationwide and provide incentives to registered owners of high polluting automobiles to replace such automobiles with new fuel efficient and less polluting automobiles." In reality it was a government-sponsored incentive program to the tune of $3 billion that helped sell 700,000 new cars. Could it work for boats? The benefits would be the same: Cleaner boats on the water and some more business for an industry that tries to emerge from the doldrums.

Well, good luck with government assistance for luxury items such as boats. Yet the thought is intriguing. A boat scrapping and recycling system also could help mitigate the nuisance of derelict boats that appeared in larger numbers during the first year of the recession when scores of boats were abandoned by their owners who were unwilling or unable to pay for their upkeep. One fellow in Washington State even sunk his yacht in Puget Sound and reported it as an accident to cash in on the insurance, but was caught. "Derelict boats are environmental and navigational hazards, leaking toxins and posing obstacles for other craft, especially at night," a story in the April 1, 2009 issue of the *New York Times* groused. "Thieves plunder them for scrap metal. In a storm, these runabouts and sailboats, cruisers and houseboats can break free or break up, causing havoc." One Florida official complained that "our waters have become dumping grounds. It's got to the point where something has to be done." There always were derelict or abandoned vessels that had to be dealt with, either by auctioning them off in lien sales to recover back taxes or marina fees or by taking them to the scrapper. But as the number of these vessels increases, so does the cost of dealing with them. And we all pay for that.

Assembly Bill 166, which was passed by the California legislature in 2008, but was left in limbo after being vetoed (along with hundreds of other bills) by Governor Arnold Schwarzenegger, proposed a pilot program to bail out boat owners, who surrender their boats to local agencies instead of abandoning them. In turn, this bill, which was co-sponsored by boating industry organizations, state government entities and environmental groups, would sharply increase fines for abandoned boats. Funding would come from the existing Abandoned Watercraft Abatement Fund. It's not quite cash for clunkers, but a step in that direction. Other states also address the issue. In South Carolina abandoning a boat on a public waterway is subject to a fine of up to $5,000 and jail. Setting up a proper disposal system that is self-sustaining by covering the cost of retrieval and disposal seems to be in the interest of the taxpayer and the environment, but it will take a collaborative effort that has overcome several challenges:

- It's expensive and complicated. Boats are big, heavy and unwieldy. "Such a system is complex to set up," Sponberg said. "Getting bigger boats out of the water needs towboats, cranes and travel lifts. Then the old boats have to be trucked to a recycling facility. Perhaps marinas could partake in such a program or federal facilities financed through vessel license fees could be set up in strategic locations."
- As it stands today, fiberglass recyclate is not highly valued, and it takes a lot of effort to extract it (see below). Then fiberglass isn't particularly toxic when it is plowed under. It just sits in the landfill and takes up space for a very long time.
- Boats are not designed and built to be recycled like cars and computers are. Hewlett Packard, like many other electronics manufacturers, offers a buyback and recycling program for consumer electronics. It also reduced the number of plastics from 200 to five and had plans to cut this number to four by eliminating polyvinyl chloride. The goal is developing products that are suitable for upgrade rather than replacement.

Reselling salvaged boat parts happens only on a small scale, i.e. at Sailorman Marine in Fort Lauderdale, Florida.

◆ We have to start calculating prices by including societal and environmental costs incurred through the current linear system that starts with resource extraction and ends with the trash heap. Once that happens, recycling and other sustainable principles will become more attractive and competitive.

While many boat manufacturers make environmental claims and state their compliance with laws and regulations, they are far less eager to quantify the results. Despite all good intentions and plans to devise a certification for eco-friendly boats, the industry is still years away from making the process more transparent and from establishing broadly accepted guidelines, similar to what OIA did with the Eco Working Group or what the EPA tries to do with Design for the Environment.

Some manufacturers are more ready to discuss these matters than others. Hanse Yachts, a German builder of sail- and powerboats, for instance, reduces VOC and styrene emissions through modern manufacturing techniques like vacuum bagging and resin infusion, which also improve the environment for workers, according to Brent Perry, vice president of motor yachts, quality assurance and customer service. "Low-VOC resins, better mold design and reduced cutting planes, all contribute to lessen waste, " Perry said, adding that the company uses alternative materials where suitable, mostly in the timber portions of the boat. Other initiatives include closed-molding lamination for large composite parts and reducing the need for copper. Furniture for Hanse's boats is produced with "60 percent less waste than a typical yard," Perry explained. Whatever scrap wood is left over fires the boilers of the factory's heating system. About fiberglass recycling he said: "Oddly enough, this is an argument for using solid laminates and organic cores. Theoretically, older boats are easier to burn (no foams) and use for things like heating. We live with the idea that our hulls and decks are so strong and well built that they will last longer, effectively improving our waste but not making it easy to recycle." To be viable, a recycling system for fiberglass boats needs tax incentives, Perry opined.

Fiberglass can be recycled in several different ways, for instance through incineration, by pyrolysis, or mechanically, by grinding it up. "Energy recovery means that you chop up the boat in smaller pieces and feed them to a heating plant," explained Hans Hansson, managing director of Swerea Sicomp AB, in Sweden. "We have done carefully controlled lab-scale experiments to study toxic products and full-scale tests in cooperation with heating plants. If you use high incineration temperatures you do not get any toxic fumes or other bi-products. However, you have to handle the ashes. The energy content is about the same as for a normal bio-fuel." How feasible FRP recycling is fiscally, depends on regulations and fees, Hansson said. Swedish companies, he pointed out, use energy recovery for production waste and save money, because they only pay for hauling it to the incinerator, when otherwise they would have to pay for disposal too, which in Hansson's words, "is not a sustainable way to take care of old boats or production waste."

Pyrolysis uses extreme temperatures and oxygen deprivation to break fiberglass down into solids, oil, and gas, all of which can be reused. The advantage of incineration and pyrolysis is that fiberglass can be "dirty," meaning it can be mixed with other substances and plastics. The drawback is that the exhaust will have to be scrubbed or otherwise treated to reduce the emission of dangerous greenhouse gasses, which isn't cheap.

Grinding up fiberglass and turning it into filler has its own set of challenges, because in laminates, woven and knitted fibers adhere to each other very well. Breaking them apart properly without destroying them is a science of its own. Coarser materials, which are better for reinforcement purposes in new construction, tend to gum up spraying equipment that is used in the laminate process, rendering it unusable. The value of the recyclate also depends on the building method of the boat. "Room-temperature-cured boat laminates tend to have unreacted catalyst in them, which, once ground up, can cause the recyclate to burst into flame by spontaneous combustion," Sponberg wrote in a story for *Professional Boatbuilder* that explored the options of fiberglass recycling. "Moreover, unreacted catalyst in a recyclate in any new product can cause its cure cycle to go haywire. Also, grinding laminates creates a lot of dust containing small fibers, which pose a serious health hazard. So the storage and handling of the recyclate has some serious remanufacturing and safety issues that need to be addressed."

Europeans are not the only ones who are in tune with FRP recycling. There are businesses in North America that are dedicated to it. Seawolf Design Inc. in New Smyrna Beach, Florida, offers consulting services, research, product design and recycling equipment to the fiberglass industry. Founder Wolfgang Unger said Seawolf developed filled-resin systems that use recyclate and noticeably lower material and labor costs, reduce or even eliminate laminate rollout, decrease VOC emissions and increase product quality. According to Seawolf, recycled FRP can be used in spray-up, putties, casting, concrete reinforcement, pre-forms, compression molding, and pultrusion to make bath tubs, spas, sinks, modular buildings, moldings and, yes, boats. The objective is to cut down on material and dumping costs. That's exactly the principle of composting kitchen scraps, except that fiberglass recycling needs a lot of energy, which also makes it expensive, while composting is free. To demonstrate that nevertheless there are meaningful uses for recycled fiberglass, Unger sent a smattering of laminate examples that all were made from recyclate. "I've been in fiberglass recycling since 1987," he said. "It's not impossible, maybe just a little complicated. Boat builders need to use it to see that they can achieve a 30-percent savings in fibers. Recyclate as bedding compound for core material increases shear resistance by 30 percent." Recycling fiberglass is also one of the businesses of R.J. Marshall Company, which claims to have processing capabilities to handle up to 5 million pounds of recyclate, The firm says it developed a method to process thermoset plastics into filler on open-loop (recyclate used in other applications) and closed-loop (recyclate used in same application) systems.

In 2008, Ashland Inc. of Dublin, Ohio, teamed up with Canadian sport boat manufacturer Campion Boats to test the Envirez resin that is formulated from soybean oil. "Materials from recycled products and renewable sources are key components of the products in Ashland's Envirez resin line . . . the first step to sustainable composites," Ashland said in a press announcement. Two of the key benefits from an environmental perspective are the reduced content of crude oil (compared to traditional resins) and hence fewer CO_2 emissions during manufacture.

Several years ago, Swerea Sicomp, Seawolf and Swedish boat builder Ryds developed a small concept boat with recycled scrap. Hansson said about 35 percent recyclate and 65 percent virgin materials were used. The recycled material was put in as core between inner and outer laminates of virgin material. "We achieved approximately the same stiffness properties for the same weight as with virgin material only. Strength properties were lower with recycled material, but good enough for the boats we used as demonstrators." The savings are a bit tricky to calculate, Hansson added, but at the very least companies save landfill disposal fees, which have gone up sharply, with the express purpose to reduce the share of landfill of the total waste. In Europe some countries have begun to restrict FRP landfill, which means that if these laws are closely enforced (they are not yet), the remnants of old fiberglass boats would have to be incinerated, pyrolized, recycled, or shipped someplace else. By contrast U.S. landfills still expand and disposal fees are comparatively cheap. Sponberg wrote that Monroe County in the Florida Keys in the late 1990s already averaged over 100 collected and disposed boats each year and spent between $1,000 to $3,000 to salvage a typical 20 to 25-foot boat. For trucking and dumping the carcasses into landfills he calculated $92 per ton, or $100 to $150 per boat on average. Considering the possibility of disposal fees of $500 to $1,000 per ton and the mountain of waste that millions of fiberglass boats will produce when they meet their ends, a functional recycling system would indeed make sense—and money.

According to a report in Boating Business, Sandy Cove Marine Recyclers, in Honey Harbour, Ontario, Canada, is collecting old fiberglass boats of up to 25 feet in length, which then are stripped and trucked to a shredding facility nearby where they are ground up. The plan was to research the use of fiberglass recyclate as insulation or as concrete filler for construction applications. The story quoted company president Don Ford saying that "so far we've grounded [sic] up over a hundred boats. I have more than 50 sitting in my yard." He indicated that there were at least 100 more he could have picked up at several marinas. The disposal fee for boats from 18 to 22 feet run at ca. CDN$300, but could be less if salvageable items can be recovered and sold. If successful, Ford hoped to secure funding from the Canadian government to set up a subsidized program for boat disposal in the region.

Could such a system become a reality in the U.S.? Not likely, experts said, at least not in the foreseeable future, even though using discarded fiberglass as feedstock for heat recovery or pyrolysis remain options. But at this point doing what's right for the environment has to wait for a boost, perhaps from government mandate or tax incentives. The other possibility is economic pressure, like an escalating oil price that would impact the cost of synthetic boatbuilding materials.

Other forms of plastic

Fiberglass is perhaps the most versatile material for building pleasure craft, but it is by no means the only one. Other forms of plastic construction such as rotomolding and thermoforming have become more sophisticated and have made inroads, especially for building lower-end dinghies and kayaks. These techniques use heat to mold plastic to the desired shape of boats and almost anything else. Making large numbers of one item with little involvement of manual labor drives down the cost per unit. Thermoforming uses plastic sheets (or films) of various thicknesses that are made pliable with heat. Draped over a male mold, these sheets are formed into shape. After a cooling period the material is trimmed before hull and deck go together. "Labor is much cheaper than for building fiberglass boats and you can churn out greater numbers in a shorter time," said Tom Derrer, the founder of Eddyline Kayaks, a company that has built about 20,000 boats from thermoformed plastic over the last 15 years. "The tooling is cheaper than that for rotational molding, because it is made from composite parts and can be replaced easily." The properties of Eddyline's thermoforming material are much closer to fiberglass than polyethylene, Derrer said, which means it's lighter and stiffer. However it isn't cheap and can't be applied to any old fiberglass hull design. "When we switched from fiberglass to thermoformed plastic, 90 percent of our designs went out the window, so we had to start over and design boats for the new material's properties." Among U.S. sailboat builders, Hunter Marine used thermoforming for the production of smaller models from 14 to 21 feet, but has discontinued the technology for cost reasons. Attempts to obtain an official statement from the company regarding this matter were unsuccessful.

The more popular method of mass production by far is rotational molding, which uses polyethylene granulate that is poured into a hollow mold where it is heated and formed into the desired shape through rotation. After a few hours these boats come out of the mold in one piece so there's no leaking hull-deck joint. Hull strength is very even and the material doesn't absorb water like old fiberglass jalopies often do. Tooling is expensive and good results require precise temperature control throughout the process, but manual labor is kept to a minimum, and it produces consistent quality with next to no waste, so it is cost effective as long as the production runs are large. There's no paint, no varnish, no gel coat and they withstand usual bumps and bruises without drama. All of which makes them ideal for resorts, clubs and rental operations or individuals who want to go boating without worrying about a brittle craft. Repairs are tricky though, because they require specific tools and skills that are not found in typical boatyards. At the end of their useful life, rotomolded PE boats can be ground up and turned into lower-grade PE products like ice fishing shacks, playground structures, cargo boxes, storage tanks, garbage cans, cattle warmers, bait stations, or skunk traps.

For a long time, rotomolding used only one layer of plastic, which was OK for entry-level boats, where weight and stiffness is less important. To make this construction technique suitable for sailboats, a three-layered process was developed to yield a lighter and stiffer structure with an inner and outer skin and a lower-density core layer, not unlike sandwich fiberglass laminate. The core layer also provides buoyancy in case the boat takes on water. Several companies have been using this process quite successfully. "Our rotomolded boats use a triple PE laminate that makes them stiffer than single-layer polyethylene kayaks," explained RS Sailing sales manager Rikki Hooker. However beneficial multi-layered PE laminates for small sailboat construction might be, they appear to be less convenient for recyclers. Neither RS Sailing nor their manufacturing contractor Rototek provided specifics in this matter. "We don't want to deal with a foam layer in the middle, because once foam is molded it changes consistency and becomes difficult to process and pulverize," said Colin Tamme, general manager of Koenders Manufacturing, a large plastic manufacturing firm in Englefeld, Saskatchewan, Canada. He prefers structures made from conventional single-layer polyethylene because they can be chipped, ground, pulverized and extruded to pellets of uniform size. "The recyclate is about 60 percent as strong as virgin material, which makes it suitable for lower-grade applications," he suggested.

Necky Kayaks of Ferndale, Washington, tried to set an example for closed-loop recycling in rotomolded boatbuilding. As the name suggests, the Manitou Recycled recreational kayaks are made from 100 percent post-industrial plastic waste that stems from Necky's manufacturing process and discarded boats. The boats weigh the same as the conventionally produced Manitou, but because the material includes recyclate, they have a muted greenish color. "We give our supplier our excess plastic and chopped boats," said Chris Heffernan, spokesman of Johnson Outdoors, Necky's parent company. "They take it back, re-extrude it, process it, and resell it to us with a little color to make it the solid green. "It allows us to recycle our excess plastic. The supplier can sell this to other people too—and anyone using polyethylene and rotomolding their boats can benefit." The company also said that it donates one percent of gross sales to the Waterkeeper Alliance. But this approach has yet to catch on with the consumer. Retail price is approximately 10 percent higher than for the regular Manitou models and consumer response has been very slow, according to Heffernan. "Accounts and the press loved the news, but sell-through has been pretty low. People want to do what's right, I just think they don't want to have to pay more for it."

So where do we go from here? Rotomolded PE kayaks and dinghies can have a smaller eco-footprint, but fiberglass still is the material of choice for most sailboats. A return to wooden boats, as some iconoclasts might prefer, is not realistic. They are labor-intensive and expensive to make. It's getting increasingly difficult to source material and keeping them fit requires a lot of sanding and painting or varnishing, neither of which helps the environment.

Sensible solutions for sailboats are complex. We still want fast, exciting and easily handled boats that are affordable to buy and maintain. Fiberglass made the sport accessible to me and millions of other people of modest means and it should continue to do that. But leaving things where they are does not address the disposal issue. By encouraging us to articulate solutions, i.e. by turning plastics into resources, David de Rothschild promotes promising ideas. But he knows that ideas alone won't get it done. "At the end we need to show quantifiable outcomes," he said about the goal of his PLASTIKI mission. And the end is a good start for addressing plastic boats, as Russell Bowler wrote in *Professional Boatbuilder*: "Starting now, designers will need to anticipate the end at the beginning."

SOURCES:
Ashland Inc.: www.ashland.com
Campion Boats: www.campionboats.com
Hanse Yachts: www.hanseyachts.com
Koenders Mfg: www.koendersmfg.com
Necky Kayaks: www.neckykayaks.com
RJ Marshall: www.rjmarshall.com
RS Boats: www.rssailing.com
Ryds Boatbuilders: www.ryds.se
Seawolf Design: www.seawolfindustries.com
Eric Sponberg Yacht Design: www.sponbergyachtdesign.com
Swerea Sicomp: www.swereasicomp.se

12

Sick Oceans, Sick Planet

"A staggering 80 percent of all the life on Earth is to be found hidden beneath the waves and this vast global ocean pulses around our world driving the natural forces which maintain life on our planet," notes the Greenpeace Web site. "The oceans provide vital sources of protein, energy, minerals and other products of use the world over and the rolling of the sea across the planet creates over half our oxygen, drives weather systems and natural flows of energy and nutrients around the world, transports water masses many times greater than all the rivers on land combined and keeps the Earth habitable. Without the global ocean there would be no life on Earth. It is gravely worrying, then, that we are damaging the oceans on a scale that is unimaginable to most people."

All earthlings are stakeholders in the effort to preserve or restore aquatic environments, hence marine conservation is a critical piece in the sustainability puzzle. Listening to scientists of various disciplines, corrective action no longer is optional, but mandatory and it will cost a lot of money. But doing nothing and hoping for the best would be far worse.

Sailors have a vested interest in preserving or improving ocean health, which makes them perfect advocates for the cause. They are familiar with the aquatic environment and have—or should have—first-hand knowledge of the issues that put pressure on the oceans, such as climate change, acidification, oil pollution, plastic garbage, sewage, toxic waste. Sailors also can and should lead by promoting sustainable thoughts and practices, share their stories with the public and especially the next generation who will have to deal with our legacy. "It's all about awareness," said Mark Schrader, a veteran ocean racer-turned-conservationist, who went to sea again as the captain of OCEAN WATCH, a 64-foot steel cutter that set out from Seattle, Washington, to circumnavigate the American continent clockwise. The expedition, known as *Around the Americas* was going to collect scientific data along the way, covering 25,000 miles in 13 months, with stops in 11 countries and 30 ports. "I was always fascinated by the high latitudes and wanted to go through the Northwest Passage, but never made it." However, global warming is likely to change that. OCEAN WATCH's route took the vessel across the Beaufort Sea along the oil-rich North Slope, and farther east into the passage as the ice receded. "Sailors say they love the water, but thus far they have not been very vocal in making positive change happen or help pass legislation that protects oceans," Schrader explained. "We want to make [this voyage] mean something and share it."

For the scientific aspects of the voyage, *Around the Americas* partnered with the University of Washington's Applied Physics Laboratory, the Joint Institute for the Study of the Atmosphere and Ocean, RMR Co., MIT Sea Grant, NASA, and Western Washington University. The expedition took a cross-disciplinary approach that wasn't limited to data collection, but integrated the findings of the onboard research with educational materials that were developed by the Pacific Science Center. The hope was to develop a K-8 teacher's guide for classroom use, and a toolkit for informal education programs. Research topics included acidification, coral reef ecology, changes in sea level, sustainable fisheries, and marine biodiversity, lessons on atmospheric aerosols, underwater sound, and sea ice. Updates about the journey were posted to the *Around the Americas* Web site, while the vessel itself served as the messenger at each stopover.

Building awareness

Joining *Around the Americas* was Sailors for the Sea, the non-profit that wants to tap the sailing demographic to take the initiative in becoming a part of the solution. SfS takes some of its cues from the Surfrider Foundation, a non-profit grassroots organization that is dedicated to the protection and enjoyment of the oceans. Founded in 1984 by a handful of surfers in Malibu, California, the Surfrider Foundation now has 50,000 members and 80 chapters worldwide. With about 200 paying members and 1000 subscribers to the e-mail newsletter, SfS has a ways to go before it reaches critical mass, but it is growing and making strides toward becoming the sailors' platform that facilitates solutions for the environment. SfS conducts the Clean Regatta program that offers three levels of certifications for race organizers, who want to cut back on waste through recycling, stormwater pollution prevention, biofuels for chase boats, reducing overall energy use, or the use of non-toxic bottom paints. In 2009, SfS took its show on the road to assist the Heineken Regatta, the BVI Spring regatta and the Antigua Race Week. While most of these measures make common sense, assuming that they are common practice is a mistake. "People want to know what they can do, but they don't know where to start," said Dan Pingaro, director of SfS. So the first order of business is education and creation of problem awareness. "We favor a non-confrontational and collaborative approach so people can pick their pace. Let them do what they are comfortable with."

Volunteerism drives positive change in individual behavior and could be the fillip to transform the marine industry through the Certified Sea Friendly program (see Chapter 1).

"How can we incentivize people to do what's right and what's within their power?" asked Susan Shingledecker, program director with the BoatU.S. Foundation, the non-profit arm of BoatU.S. The organization started as the BoatU.S. Foundation for Safety in 1981, to which the environmental mission was added in 1993. Like most of the non-profits it is funded by donations and grants, but also by the mighty BoatU.S. Association, which has 600,000 members who donate on average $4 each. The operating budget of approximately $1.5 million is largely spent on safety programs, with ca. 30 percent set aside for clean-water initiatives. The educational efforts include free brochures, the Web site, but increasingly also new media like YouTube, social networks, and podcasts. The foundation also tests boating products, such as biodegradable boat cleaners, then publishes the findings in magazine and online articles.

"We also make Clean Water grant programs available to local groups, or scale local initiatives to a national level," Shingledecker explained. "We received a grant request for recycling fishing lines to keep old lines out of the water and prevent entanglements and harm to marine life. What started with education eventually became a national program with 750 containers that were sent to groups around the country who collect old fishing lines." The BoatU.S. Foundation also has been part of the Clean Marina program, which is administered by the states. The main role is facilitating information exchange about best practices. However, the program is under-funded and does not exist in inland states, since it is linked to NOAA coastal management program. The organization also was in the process of developing an interactive map of existing pump-out stations in the Northeast. This sounded like a great idea for other popular boating venues as well, where pumping raw sewage overboard impacts water quality. But for the time being, a shortage of funds limited the scope of this project to New England. "Pleasure boaters are a part of the big picture," Shingledecker explained. "Sometimes they get the brunt of the blame when they are not the bulk of the problem. Still, we have to help keep the industry clean and continue to educate participants."

Looking across the Big Pond, the pied piper for eco-conscious boating is the Green Blue in the U.K. It is an environmental awareness initiative by the British Marine Federation and the Royal Yachting Association that promotes the sustainable use of coastal and inland waters, and the sustainable operation and development of the recreational boating industry. The focus is on six areas: oil and fuel, cleaning and maintenance, antifouling and marine paints, waste management, resource efficiency and effects on wildlife. The organization, which serves as a model for many fledgling environmental boating non-profits in the U.S., targets recreational boaters and their organizations through a differentiated approach based on academic research and sophisticated polling methods. "We split the audience and therefore the messaging," said project manager Sarah Black. "First the boaters, then the industries that support the sector. The boaters are split into inland and coastal boaters, then into power and sail, then further into inflatables and personal water craft operators." To reach marine industry businesses, the Green Blue works with the British Marine Federation and its associations, promoting the cost savings for businesses and clubs that result from picking the "low-hanging fruit" by turning off lights, reducing leaks from taps and hoses, improving energy efficiency etc. Once that's accomplished, the focus shifts to innovations that produce economic advantages, solutions such as eco-friendly cleaning products, spill-proof fuel canisters, recycled plastic products that help improve sales and are featured on a separate Web site.

Black considers legislation an expensive and ineffective tool. "There are enough measures out there, but they are not enforced, creating more would probably not help." Instead, she favors the voluntary approach. The best environmental practices help manage risks, save costs and build a market advantage. "In seven months our recycling officer has helped marine industries divert more than 1.6 million gallons of waste from landfill to recycling, saving more than £45,000 for the industry."

To address boaters directly, the Green Blue uses face-to-face communication, publications, talks, and practical projects on the ground. The organization leverages the RYA yacht master instructors' syllabus and works through boat brokers and marina operators to reach berth holders. What's most effective? The direct and personal approach, because, as Black emphasized, "seeing is believing." It takes patience and persistence, that's why the Green Blue favors a measured approach. The goal is to educate and inform boaters *and* the boating industry about the environmental impacts of their activity, accompanied by constructive suggestions on how to minimize impact in incremental steps. "By working towards an environmentally self-regulating boating community, we can save money, avoid red tape and safeguard the waters and habitats we enjoy for the future."

Conservation education

Another facet of educating the public and building awareness about the deteriorating health of oceans and waterways is the integration of sailing in the curriculum. "Up to 40 percent of our guests have never sailed before," said Dave Robinson, director of Sealife Conservation, a non-profit that is supported by West Marine founder Randy Repass and offers educational trips on the DEREK M BAYLIS, a 65-foot Wyliecat ketch through the Sailing Adventures program at the Monterey Aquarium. Sealife Conservation also works with the Boy Scouts, the Boy & Girls Club and educational organizations. In

Photo 12.1 Aboard the DEREK M BAYLIS, educator Hannah Campbell teaches students about the microscopically small contents of the water column. *Dieter Loibner*

the fall, it helps with a great white shark tagging program in the Farallon Islands, west of San Francisco. More recently, the DEREK M BAYLIS also conducted marine debris research on San Francisco Bay with a geographic information system mapping tool and shared the findings with organizations such as the Regional Water Quality Control Board and the Ocean Protection Council. "We date and analyze it, with position found, when found, estimated age and type of debris and we try to identify the source," Robinson said. "People have to be able to see their impact, it's nearly personalizing [trash]."

O'Neill Sea Odyssey in Santa Cruz, California is an educational program that uses a 65-foot sailing catamaran to teach to fourth- to sixth-grade students from schools in the region three subjects: marine science, marine and watershed ecology, and navigation/mathematics. "We are part of the ocean-literacy movement," says executive director Dan Haifley. "It's a glaring omission that most [school] curricula don't use ocean concepts, which are vital to all of life on Earth. It is the base of natural and physical science." With more than 50,000 students who have participated since the program's inception in 1996, O'Neill Sea Odyssey has become a fixture for schools in the region. The program's curriculum supports the educational goals of the participating schools, and aligns with state and federal education standards. In 2005 Sea Odyssey received the California Governor's award in Economic and Environmental Leadership and U.S. Senator Barbara Boxer's Conservation Champion award. In addition, Sea Odyssey also provides a program for cognitively and physically challenged individuals. But the program has other benefits as well. "Part of the predicament [for the schools] is that the No Child Left Behind act eliminated field trips," Haifley said. "We bend over backwards to help teachers get kids out on the water, because you can't protect what you don't understand."

But non-profits are not limited to purely educational roles. Cooperating with commercial outfits to raise money for environmental causes, for instance, can bring about positive change in ecologically sensitive areas. In places where cash is scarce and indigenous people often are forced to exploit limited natural resources to eke out a living, that can make a big difference. One such example is a charter trip that was organized by Olympic Circle Sailing Club in Berkeley, California, in 2002. Members chartered a dozen catamarans from The Moorings in Placentia, Belize. Instead of pocketing the discount OCSC and the sailors decided to donate the money to the Toledo Institute for Development and the Environment (TIDE), a local grassroots environmental organization. More than $6,000 helped repair hurricane damage to a Ranger Station in the Port Honduras Marine Reserve that stands guard to prevent incursions by manatee poachers. In addition to developing sustainable use of Belize's natural resources, TIDE also educates fishermen to generate indirect income from one of the world's largest and healthiest barrier reef as guides for snorkel and kayaking trips and as fly fishing instructors. Armed with firsthand knowledge, Belizean fishermen helped train their peers on Long Island Sound on how to become caretakers of the environment. The donation was facilitated by Seacology, a Berkeley based non-profit organization that specializes in the preservation of threatened island habitats and cultures. "By becoming the first sailing club to work with us, OCSC set an example," said Seacology's executive director, Duane Silverstein. "We applaud them for helping sailors protect the marine environment while doing what they love most." Later, OCSC made similar donations to non-profits in other charter destinations, including Ocean Spirits in Grenada and Archelon in Greece, two

Photo 12.2 New anchoring systems like the Australian EzyRider use large buoys and shock cords to keep the chains above the seafloor, thus protecting coral and beds of sea grass. *EzyRider*

organizations that work to protect sea turtles. Other charitable contributions went to the British Virgin Islands National Parks Trust and the relief efforts following the devastating tsunami in the Indian Ocean in 2004.

"Successful conservation only happens when locals are involved and derive the benefits," Silverstein said. "It's not just the right thing but it's the only way that conservation will work." Seacology is not directly involved with sailing organizations but focused exclusively on island environments and cultures. The organization is looking for win-win projects that give islanders something tangible in exchange of establishing a marine or forest preserve. Thus far, Seacology has conducted more than 180 projects on 103 islands in 45 different countries. Projects use money from donors and donated labor from locals, so each dollar goes far, Silverstein explained. For $25,000, a school can be built and a marine preserve can be established.

"Sailors can insist that charter companies support the deployment of more mooring buoys in sensitive coral reef areas and the construction of pump-out stations to empty holding tanks" Silverstein suggested. "Mooring buoys are especially important because an anchor that is dropped onto a coral reef will not only destroy the area of its initial impact, but has a much bigger footprint, i.e. when it drags or the boat swings around and drags the chain across coral heads. It takes years for a healthy reef to regenerate itself."

SOURCES:
Around the Americas: www.aroundtheamericas.org
BoatU.S. www.boatus.com/foundation
The Green Blue/UK: www.thegreenblue.org.uk,
    www.sailingnetworks.com/green
Greenpeace Web site: www.greenpeace.org/international/
    campaigns/oceans
Olympic Circle Sailing Club: www.ocsc.com
O'Neill Sea Odyssey: www.oneillseaodyssey.org
Sailors for the Sea: www.sailorsforthesea.org
Save Our Shores: www.saveourshores.org
Sealife Conservation www.sealifeconservation.org
Surfrider Foundation: www.surfrider.org
Seacology: www.seacology.org

13

Miscellaneous Virtues

"Wear sunscreen. If I could offer you only one tip for the future, sunscreen would be it." Thus started a column of Chicago Tribune writer Mary Schmich, which was mistaken for a commencement speech and later became a book (*Wear Sunscreen: A Primer for Real Life*), and a hit song. For us sailing folks at least, sunscreen is as routine as brushing teeth. Prominent sailors shared their sunscreen secrets in the Sailing Scuttlebutt newsletter. There were as many different products as there are boats to sail: lotions, potions, rash guards, mineral creams, and sun protection factors you'd never heard of. The bottom line: Don't leave the dock without it. Put it on an hour before you leave. Chris Larson, a 1997 Rolex Yachtsman of the Year blogged about actinic keratosis (pre-cancers), and biopsies, lip laser resurfacing and a chemical face peel. "Trust me, these are not things you want to experience . . ." It's the dark side of the sun and a grave concern for all outdoor enthusiasts, but especially water rats. "Application is *absolutely* the most important factor in sun protection," Larson implored.

After some contemplation, I started to feel guilty, because I haven't spent a great deal of time pondering the intricacies of sunscreen. Get one with a high protection factor that's waterproof and doesn't burn in the eyes. Slap it on, rub it in, and forget about it. But that's changing. I learned that even the most sophisticated products could have undesired side effects that are not yet fully understood. So maybe sunscreen isn't that good after all? I also never worried about what happens with sunscreen after I take a shower and wash this stuff off. Down the drain, end of story, right? Not so fast. That's when sunscreen enters the next phase of its existence. It leaves our skin, but it stays in the environment. In January 2008, National Geographic wrote about a study that appeared in the journal Environmental Health Perspectives and estimated that worldwide 4,000 to 6,000 *metric tons* of sunscreen slough off swimmers in oceans every year. As a consequence, up to 10 percent of coral reefs are threatened by bleaching, because chemical sunscreen ingredients can awaken dormant viruses in the symbiotic algae that live inside corals. Researchers found that even low concentrations of sunscreen could activate these viruses and bleach coral within days. Seawater surrounding the coral that were exposed to sunscreen contained up to 15 times more viruses than unexposed samples. The tested sunscreen brands had four ingredients in common: paraben, cinnamate, benzophenone, and a camphor derivative. The findings are not undisputed in the scientific community, so the discussion is ongoing. The solution, one scientist suggested, is not a ban of sunscreen, but the conscious choice of products, i.e. sunscreens that have physical filters to reflect ultraviolet radiation and use eco-friendly ingredients.

But that's not necessarily enough, either. Environmental Health News carried a report about University of Toledo researchers who discovered that nano-titanium dioxide, which is used in sunscreens and other cosmetic products, impacts the biological functions of bacteria. These particles, which end up at municipal sewage treatment plants with the run-off from showers, could eliminate microbes that play vital roles in ecosystems and help treat wastewater by removing ammonia from wastewater treatment systems, cleaning up toxic waste and reducing phosphorus in lakes. I asked a representative from the Bureau of Environmental Services in Portland, Oregon, if this claim is credible. "Yes, absolutely. It is especially bad on hot summer days, when people use a lot of sunscreen which then shows up in municipal wastewater." Another study conducted by scientists of Utah State University and the University of Utah suggested that beneficial soil bacteria also have trouble dealing with common sunscreen ingredients like silver, copper and zinc oxide. The researchers warned these particles could be toxic to aquatic life since it takes only a tiny dose, the equivalent to two drops in an Olympic-size swimming pool to produce damage in bacteria. These and other findings point to the uncertainty about the risks and benefits of nanoparticles in consumer products, because research has yet to catch up to their rising popularity.

Is there a product that prevents skin cancer from exposure and won't kill the corals? The best advice is consulting a dermatologist and doing some legwork to find which product works for your skin *and* the algae of the coral reefs. I have started a personal trial with Melansol, an antioxidant sunscreen that supports my body's own defense mechanism against sunburn and chronic UV damage. The product uses mineral pigments like zinc oxide and a small amount of titanium dioxide to reflect the UV rays rather than chemical UV filters. It contains no alcohol, has not undergone animal testing and is compliant with FDA regulations, according to Oceana Naturals, the U.S. distributor. Supposedly it's also safe for the environment, because it's biodegradable and does not contain chemicals that break down in UV rays and pollute the water. The highest SPF rating is 25, about half what others offer. High SPF ratings, the Web site explains, "give the wrong message and a false sense of security. People are led to believe that they can apply a high SPF sunscreen and proceed to spend an unlimited amount of time in the sun." It will take a season on the water to collect enough anecdotal evidence about the effectiveness of the product. So far I've been religious in applying it: It goes on easy and penetrates the skin quickly. It doesn't smell offensively and it doesn't sting the eyes when sweating. It also was approved by my daughter, which is important, because kids don't think of sunscreen as a necessity. But if they form useful habits they'll be better off later. Back to Mary Schmich's advice: "Wear sunscreen. Stretch. Do one thing every day that scares you." Agreed. But let's hope that wearing sunscreen itself won't become a scary thing.

Folding a bike

In my efforts to lighten the carbon load, I discovered that there's nothing like fun to breed positive habits that deliver collateral benefits. A few years ago I was looking for cheap transportation during a magazine assignment in Europe. Distances typically are short over there but parking almost always is a nightmare. At the time gas was close to $8 a gallon and a rental car would have added another fat line item to the expense report that would have turned this venture into a tough proposition. I discussed it with the editor, who has a soft spot for folding bikes. "You ought to try one of those," he suggested. A folder? What the hell am I going to do with a folding bike? Renting a full-sized bicycle sure would be easier, but that's always a crapshoot, especially in Europe in the summer. So I started to research this field and chose a Dahon Mariner D7, which is a basic model that was designed for boaters, even though it is listed as a urban utility bike. It has 7 gears, a brushed aluminum frame, stainless-steel spokes, a rust-resistant chain, fenders and a rack. I owed it to the cause to show up with a bike that had a boat theme built in. The Mariner also has 20-inch wheels, so it doesn't fold as compactly as a 16-inch model, but larger wheels are more comfortable on uneven terrain or on cobblestone streets. I added a packing case that turned the bike into a piece of luggage, fit to be taken on a plane, albeit at extra cost.

Before the trip I had a few weeks to get used to the vehicle, practicing the folding and unfolding routines, which require memorizing three or four steps and a little bit of finger strength. Converting a bicycle to a jumble of spokes and tubes in less than half a minute often drew an audience of people who marveled at the simplicity of the process. Riding the bike was also a trip and a social experience. The upright posture was very comfortable and an asset for navigating city traffic. The short wheelbase made it fun to whip around tight corners and going fast wasn't out of the question, but required more work, due to the small number of gears, the upright position (wind resistance!), and the small wheels that travel nearly 25 percent less distance per turn than a full-sized bike. Adding clip pedals that transfer muscle power better to the road helped uphill.

There are hundreds of folding bikes on the market, and quite sophisticated (and pricey) ones at that. But a bike has to have the right kind of utility to be useful and the Mariner was well within my expectations and budget, which is why it became the favorite two-wheeler in my garage. At 25 pounds it can't be called a featherweight, but it's light enough to be carried on a bus or lugged around an airport. With a packing size of 11 x 31 x 26 inches, it takes a deep lazarette to stow it out of the way or some serious cabin space, which is an issue on smaller boats. But it's not all fun and games. A folding bike needs regular maintenance: A drop of oil for the hinges, tightening the levers, adjusting the break and shifter cables, rotating tires and replacing the brake pads are simple enough for a regular DIY service schedule.

Photo 13.1 Although not the most compact collapsible bike available, the Dahon Mariner tucks into a regular boat lazarette or car trunk when folded. A separate carrying case is available for air travel. *Dahon*

Aside from utility, the social aspect of riding a folder was new to me. Hardly an outing went by without people asking questions or commenting on the unusual looks. Before I realized it, the queer adventure of riding a folding bike became a healthy habit, because now I have wheels whenever and wherever I want: in the trunk of the car, on a boat, on a bus, on a train, and on a plane. I ride more because I can combine various modes of transportation. It makes me more flexible and independent and I can get around faster without burning any gas: to the farmer's market, to the sailing club, on to the ferry (bypassing the long line of cars), huffing and puffing up the 10,000-foot Tioga Pass in Yosemite, taking it on a boat delivery, pedaling to the gates of a boat show and getting primo parking for free. The possibilities are endless. Not to forget the cool factor and the saved expenses on that assignment in Europe. One morning as I pedaled to the job site, I remembered Stuart Alexander, whom I met during the America's Cup of 1995 in San Diego. A veteran sailing reporter, he was there for the U.K. newspaper *Independent* and made a deep impression. Rain or shine, he rode his bike around Shelter

Island to the team bases and the media center. I didn't quite understand this devotion to pedals then, but I'm a convert now.

Pros:

- Portability and versatility
- Compact enough to be stowed on boats
- Wheels when you want them, where you want them
- Combining workout with zero-emission transport

Photo 13.2 The author on a zero-emission trip with a Dahon Mariner M7 folding bike, and a Walker Bay Airis inflatable kayak in the backpack. *Dieter Loibner*

Cons:
- Not as efficient as a rigid 27-inch bike
- Requires more work especially uphill
- More maintenance

SOURCES
Bike Friday: www.bikefriday.com
Dahon: www.dahon.com
Downtube: www.downtube.com
Transportation Alternatives: www.transalt.org/resources/
    foldingbikes

Fractional ownership

Spend a joyful day on the water. Get back, tie up, walk away and let someone else worry about the rest. Welcome to fractional sailing, an idea that aims to take the burden of ownership by dividing the cost and increasing the use. Paying less is good, using boats that otherwise would be sitting idle is good, and sailing is golden. It's a win-win-win situation that improves efficiency—and sustainability.

Fractional sailing is a spin of the timeshare/charter concept. Some vendors own the boats and provide their members with varying levels of access in different locations. Others operate on a franchise basis, either owning the boats that get rented to club members, or selling boats and leasing them back from their owners, and adding shareholders who pay an annual fee for guaranteed usage. The third variation caters to people who *want* to own a boat, just not all of it.

Cutting costs and increasing the use of boats that are dock-bound most of their life is an appealing idea from an economic and ecological perspective. To some, the timeshare/charter model is a means to help grow the sport, because it is a sensible lifestyle choice. "People will be looking to gather experiences in the future rather than assets," said George Benelli, CEO of SailTime. "Fractional programs will take advantage of that continued shift in the consumer marketplace and I believe [they] can bring the joys of being on the water with friends and family to a much wider audience." And he's not alone with this opinion. "It's a no-brainer," agreed Grant Headifen with Nautic 7, a veteran of the fractional boating business who started SailTime and now manages the fractional ownership program for Beneteau. "It is the way of the future. People who want to get into boating ask themselves, 'do I have time and do I have the money?' People who have lost a good chunk of their investments and retirement money [during the recession] will have to work longer and make due with less." Tying up money with one asset is silly, he said, but with fractional ownership people get all the fun but only half the bills.

Beneteau said it sees fractional yachting as a way of opening the sport to newcomers who like the sport but might not (yet) be fully aware of the scope of responsibilities. And technology can make a big difference: Booking and billing are all done online. Before leaving the dock, a skipper must complete a comprehensive checklist on a smart phone that is immediately sent back to Nautic 7, indicating the condition of the boat. If another co-owner constantly leaves behind a mess, or returns the boat dinged up, the next operator will report it. "By signing the owners' contract, you agree to pay a fine for repeated violations and that money goes into the boat's kitty," Headifen explained. Nautic 7 also put sailing courses online, so members can cram for the license when and where they want.

Trading a share of the expenses for time they don't use their boat, appeals to owners who want to create income to offset some of the cost. At Etap Charter Lease, based in Stamford, Connecticut, seven shareholders pay a flat annual fee to use a privately owned Etap 37. Each gets two weeks per season. "It is a compelling model for owners who don't use their boat full time and for individuals who don't need or want ownership," said Ludwig Hoogstoel of Etap USA. A calculation on the company's Web site showed a cost of a little over $400 per day for shareholders vs. more than $2,200 for the same boat if it is owned outright by a single individual, assuming 6 percent interest on a 20-year loan.

However, fractional sailing is not for everybody and owners who see their boat as more than just a tool that takes them out on the water will probably agree. Making an appointment to go sailing ahead of time takes the element of spontaneity out of it. What if the weather is bad? What if the crew isn't available? Then there's the vanity factor. Privately owned boats often are status symbols that inform about their owners in a way that charter boats never can. Pride of ownership: Sometimes this means picking up a wrench, a sheet of sand paper, a caulking gun and a paintbrush. It's part of bonding with the boat. Trust: Putting a private boat in charter, one has to trust the managing company's assessment of their clients' sailing abilities. The same is true for shared ownership. Will the other fellows be careful with the boat or will you spend all your time sorting out conflicts? Fractional ownership models like Beneteau's that call for four parties per boat can be a tough sell, especially in a down-economy, because it requires four times the sales effort for the dealer. The Moorings said it has shelved its factional program, but still offers the guaranteed revenue option that gives owners a maximum of nine weeks per year aboard their boat, while it is in charter service the rest of the time, earning a monthly check, which helps cover the owner's costs.

Still, the concept of fractional sailing can help beginners get started and keep others happy who just want to go sailing without the burden of ownership. "People today have many competing interests and fractional boating accommodates this lifestyle," said Paula Nelson, owner of the SailTime franchise in Annapolis, Md. "You go boating when you want, hassle-free. You won't feel guilty about not using your boat enough or using it too often, thus neglecting other commitments."

SOURCES:
Beneteau Fractional: www.beneteaufractional.com
Etap Charter Lease: www.etapcharterlease.com
Nautic 7: www.nautic7.com
The Moorings: www.moorings.com
Pinnacle Yachts: www.pinnacleyachts.com
SailTime: www.sailtime.com
Wind Path: www.windpath.com

Reviving tattered sails

There used to be two things that were certain in life: Death and taxes. Now there's a third: Junk. Cleaning out the basement of my parents' house in Austria after my father had passed away and my mom had moved to a care facility, brought to light a ton of detritus from times long gone, including an old Dacron Finn Dinghy sail. It was way past its prime when I sold my last boat a lifetime ago, but for some reason it didn't get trashed. So it sat and collected dust for

20 years. Finally it had to go. I think one of the Chechen asylum seekers, who got wind of my doings and came by to pick through the pile, might have taken it. Whatever he needed it for, I'm sure it wasn't sailing.

Not all societies have reached the troubling decadence of the industrial nations where the last stop for almost everything is the scrap heap. Repairing or re-using, which used to be part of the waste-not-want-not philosophy, is becoming increasingly difficult, because products are designed for planned obsolescence. Sails are no different. Once they loose the ability to hold their shape well, they get demoted from racing to a leisure sailing. But at one point it has to be retired for good, then what? "It ends up in the garage," said designer Tom Wylie. "That's the penultimate stop before it becomes landfill."

Out of curiosity I kicked around some numbers. The Laser arguably is one of the most popular sailing vessels ever built. It has only one sail that measures ca. 76 square feet. The number of Lasers is approaching 200,000. That's 15.2 million square feet of Dacron, if each boat had only one sail. But that is not the case. Since many Lasers are being raced, the skippers usually have at least two sets of sails. I heard of professionals who go through as many as a dozen of them every year, using a new sail for every major regatta. Assuming that five percent of all Lasers built (i.e. 10,000) are or were raced and their skippers bought two new sails in addition to the original set, adds another 1.52 million square feet. Now we are looking at 16.72 million square feet of sail that are destined for the trash. And that's just for Lasers.

According to the 2007 Boating Abstract by the National Marine Manufacturers Association, there are approximately 17 million pleasure boats in use in the U.S., 1.55 million of them sailboats. Assuming an average sail area of 250 square feet (without spinnaker) means these boats would have a combined sail area of nearly 390 million square feet or nearly 14 square miles, which is the equivalent of 6,700 football fields. That's if they only have one set of sails. Once these sails are done, where do they go? Dacron, and more modern fibers or laminates such as Mylar, Kevlar, Spectra and carbon fiber have many desirable properties, but they are not known for being biodegradable.

However, the thought of reusing old and tired sails is not far fetched. Several outfits are actively engaging in this practice and have had success in turning old sails into products that have market value. "The idea of recycling sails is one we've had in the back of our minds for over a decade," said Mark Turner of the Reefer Sail Company in the U.K. As a passionate sailor and hang glider he always hoarded old kit for posterity and the ultimate benefit of the local mouse population. "Whenever I've asked friends and colleagues who sail, what they've done with [old sails] they invariably admit they threw them away," Turner said. "Conversations with sailmakers are along the same lines. The inevitable collection of old sails usually ends up in a refuse 'skip', some go to local schools for art/performing arts projects, some for ad-hoc garden shade sails. In the U.K., entry into the regular refuse stream will turn the sail into landfill, there is no reclamation scheme for this type of textile in this country." Using mostly Dacron and rip-stop spinnaker nylon, Reefer Sail Company turns old sails into soft furnishings like cushions, bean bags, chairs, shower curtains and pet beds, but also into beach accessories, hammocks and shade sails. Turner said he's also developing a range of luggage and travel products. In addition to donated sails he recycles scraps from sailmakers and uses roll ends from sailcloth wholesalers for some products. "We never say no to the offer of a sail and can usually make something from part of it. All of our sails have to be laundered, and most interior applications require fire proofing to comply with furnishing regulations. This makes the raw material more expensive than new sailcloth off the roll, but of course the products have much more character. We also allude to the provenance of the sail in the branding we apply to the recycled sail, which we believe adds both interest and artistic value, too."

For Ella Vickers, the career path went from sailing to sail recycling at her company, Ella Vickers Recycled Sailcloth Collection. Having sailed "everything from a J/24 to an 80-foot catamaran," she knows the different varieties of the sport and the sails that are being used for it. Crewing on the 12-Meter Columbia was her favorite, even though she was chosen to go to the top every day and lash the sail head around the mast so it would not rip out. Then she would have to go back up and unlash it before the sail could be taken down.

Instead of hanging out at high altitude, she now recasts old Dacron in a new role, as shopping bags, purses and other accessories.

Photo 13.3 Ella Vickers is one of several companies that turned used sails into fashionable accessories such as bags or furniture. *Ella Vickers*

Sourcing the material is not difficult, she said. "I get a lot of sails from lofts that offer a discount for people who bring in their old sails to get new ones made, then I buy the old sails at that discount, so the loft still makes the same money." It's a good deal for both sides. She also said she buys used sails and gets tattered ones from individuals as trade-ins for bags. Sourcing partners include Intensity Sails, a specialty shop that's owned and operated by one-design sailors in Warwick, Rhode Island, and Bacon Sails in Annapolis, Maryland.

"We wash, bleach and press them if we need to, to get them white again. We also give bags to sailing schools to sell and raise money for their schools, and they give us their worn out sails." Vickers estimates that her firm helps to keep 20,000 square feet of Dacron out of the landfill each year. It won't keep the Dacron out for good, but it is a commendable contribution to the second law of sustainability, which advocates reuse. And her customers dig it. "I only get gracious positive feedback on my sailcloth collection," Vickers said. So she has created another example of a win-win-win situation by taking used cloth off the sailmakers' or the sailors' hands, by reducing the amount of trash that goes into the landfill and by selling a unique product that resonates with her clientele.

A similar deal was offered by North Sails North America, which is part of the world's largest sail making company. They called it "Think Green, Buy Blue," referring to their dominant corporate color. Customers could register to recycle their old sails and get a 25-percent discount for certain new sails. North also offered to pay the shipping of the old canvas and threw in a free tote bag from Sea Bags, Inc.

SOURCES:
Recyclers
Ella Vickers Recycled Sail Collection: www.ellavickers.com
The Reefer Sail Company: www.reefersails.com
Sea Bags, Inc. www.seabags.com
Bacon Sails: www.baconsails.com
Intensity Sails: www.intensitysails.com

LED lighting

Light emitting diode (LED) is the new wunderkind of climate-saving technologies. It's used at Buckingham Palace and on the streets of U.S. cities, but we all know it from our entertainment electronics, computers, perhaps the taillights of newer cars, and as cabin or running lights on boats. And that's just the start. LED lights are nearly a sustainability homerun with the bases loaded: They don't waste heat and can use up to 90 percent less energy than the old incandescent light bulbs. They tolerate dirt and vibration, and they are compact. They don't contain toxics and last anywhere from 30,000 to 100,000 hours (depending on application), the equivalent of 5 to 20 years of use. Something that lasts so long and consumes so little deserves a sustainability label. With one caveat: The entire system has to be properly designed and the lights need to be well made.

LEDs are tiny sandwiches of two different materials that release light as electrons jump from one to the other. The principle was discovered more than 100 years ago, and some LEDs began to see use in computers as indicator lights in the 1960s. Now, thanks to advances in technology, they have become fit for the mainstream faster than anyone anticipated, because they lost bad habits and learned new tricks. The white light lost its annoying blue tint, they can be dimmed, they can be directed, and they don't emit UV light, so they won't attract bugs, which sailors and other outdoorsy folks really appreciate.

"At first they did not have the color or the output and were only used by energy-conscious individuals, mostly as courtesy lights for outside," explained Kinder Woodcock, a product manager at Imtra, a company that produces lighting systems. "But with high-powered LEDs the light color has improved." Sailors, Woodcock said, are especially fond of this technology because it effectively addresses the notorious electricity shortage on smaller boats that do not have generators. "Sailboat guys are very energy-conscious, so LEDs are a godsend to them, because they consume much less energy, which means they can keep the battery charged with a solar panel instead of having to run the engine." Designers, too are beginning to integrate LEDs, according to Woodcock, taking advantage of their efficiency, which allows them to save weight on battery banks, wiring (as soon as the American Boat and Yacht Council updates the standards) and the size of the generator. Kinder said that ca. 70 percent of his company's sales are made up by LEDs. There are several nautical LED applications besides courtesy lighting: Trailer sailors love them, because LEDs don't have filaments that can break, they don't emit heat so they don't suffer immersion shock if the boat is launched in cold water, and they are immune to corrosion because they're sealed in a watertight plastic housing. Because LEDs are low-maintenance, more and more boaters install them as running lights, especially on the masthead but also as underwater lights. Is it possible to replace old lights? "You can replace halogens or incandescents in older fixtures with LED bulbs, which is relatively inexpensive," Kinder said. "But they are less effective and susceptible to voltage spikes, so their lifespan is less than rated."

The downside of LED is that prices remain stubbornly high. While government money motivates cities and homeowners to install these lights, boaters don't get that benefit. Paying 10 or 15 times more for an LED than for a regular bulb is stiff. It might take 10 or 15 years to recoup the cost with the energy savings and a few years less if the replacement bulbs are factored in. But such calculations are skewed, because they do not take into account the cost of electricity, which will keep rising. "Prices haven't decreased as hoped, because technology has improved," Kinder said. "Cost per lumen has come down, but not the cost of the fixtures or bulbs, because they got more sophisticated."

Still, LEDs stand to revolutionize our energy budgets and especially the electric systems on small boats. One word of caution, though: The technology, as cool as it is, also is more complex, because LED bulbs need a power supply with regulated output and special fuses.

The best white LED products can meet or exceed the efficiency of compact fluorescent lamps (CFLs), the Department of Energy's Web site stated. "However, many white LEDs currently available in consumer products are only marginally more efficient than incandescent lamps . . . Good LED system and luminaire design is imperative to energy-efficient LED lighting fixtures." In other words, it pays to hire a certified marine electrician to assist with the conversion from incandescent lights to LEDs, and to confirm that the installed lights are Coast Guard approved, so the return on investment is ensured.

Pros:
◆ Efficiency
◆ Waterproof
◆ Robust
◆ No heat emission
◆ Virtually maintenance free
◆ No toxic contents (i.e. mercury)

Cons:
◆ Price
◆ Power supply installation
◆ Produce only directional light

SOURCES:
Imtra: www.imtra.com
Hella Marine: www.hellamarine.com
US Department of Energy: www.energy.gov

14

Sustainable Cruising

Most of what has been discussed in this book has been done in the context of casual daysailing, weekend cruising or sailing while on vacation. But for a reality check there's nothing quite like getting it from the horse's mouth, meaning from the perspective of veteran cruisers who have been around at least once and know how to operate on thin air, a tight budget and a few good practices. Being on the boat 24/7 (or just about) is quite a different lifestyle that requires other habits than tying up at the dock at sunset, rinsing off the boat, throwing back a couple of cold ones and driving home to repeat the whole sequence one week later.

One of my interview subjects was Wolfgang Hausner, the longtime cruiser and catamaran sailor. After finishing school, he left his home, Austria, in the mid 1960s with a one-way ticket to the place that was farthest away for the price he could afford: Australia. He worked as a croc hunter, a lobsterman and in uranium mines to scrape together the funds he needed to build a 37-foot catamaran, which he sailed around the world alone, becoming the first singlehander to do that. Setting records wasn't his thing, but stopping to smell the roses and exploring the islands and dropping the hook when and where it pleased him. It's called slow sailing, which has nothing to do with sailing slow. Forty years and two shipwrecks later (none of his fault), he's still at it, mostly in Southeast Asia.

Then there is Commodore Warwick Tompkins, the Master Mariner par excellence, who left at age 71 with his new bride to go cruising in the South Pacific and add to his portfolio that includes a trip around the Horn at age 4 and half a million assorted sea miles as a racer and delivery captain.

The third voice comes from Doris Renoldner and Wolfgang Slanec, who took the cover shot for this book. The two, known as Sea Nomads, just returned from their second world cruise, a seven-year affair that took them to Tierra del Fuego, around some of the Great Capes, through the South Pacific and back home to Europe. They also support the Okaburura Community School on the island of Kitava in Papua New Guinea.

It is a special pleasure to include some notes from the blog of Tania Aebi, who retraced her steps from her epic solo voyage in the 1980s more than 20 years later, as a mom with her two teenage sons. It's not just instructional for would-be cruisers, but also for parents who are looking to enrich their children's education.

Lastly I will use some quotes from Cap'n Fatty Goodlander, the cruising icon, who found the time to answer probing questions about sustainable practices with candor and humor. Each one of these distinguished cruisers has a different take on the details, but in the big picture they live by the same denominator: Common sense.

Preparing for an ocean crossing

In 1996, Tompkins and pathologist Bill Siegel, both in their mid-sixties at the time, raced MUSTANG SALLY, Siegel's 30-foot Wyliecat from San Francisco to Hawaii in the West Marine Pacific Cup. They covered the course of roughly 2,100 miles in 12 days and 12 hours, which is a remarkable achievement, given the age of the crew and the size of the boat, which had only one 430-square foot main-sail and 25 feet of waterline. Yet the real puzzler is that MUSTANG SALLY was as KISS as boats come: a daysailer without inboard en-gine, reefer and generator. Tompkins took it upon himself to kit out the boat for this passage as required by the racing rules, but without loading her down to the gills. Here are some of his tricks: "Keeping weight to a minimum was important," he said. "Espe-cially with the burden of the 30 gallons of water we had to carry at the start and the reserve of 2.5 gallons we had to present at the fin-ish." He built a shelf that could hold six 5-gallon plastic bottles on the starboard side, so the load acted as ballast for the race which is mostly sailed on starboard tack. He also added a watermaker, just in case. Next he established the electrical budget for the energy loads, which were few and far between: running lights, Windex, compass light, cabin lights, autopilot, watermaker, weatherfax and SSB radio. They were fed with one 8-D battery trickle-charged with three solar panels. For the galley he added a small self-gimbaling propane stove, a large plastic cooler with wet and dry ice, and some plastic storage bins for the larder. All in all, Tompkins reckoned, he'd added less than 1,000 pounds in gear and supplies to make it to Hawaii and back. "The boat was well balanced, which helped us in many ways," he said. "It was easy to sail downwind, which conserved energy, because the autopilot didn't have to work hard." On the way to the islands, all was well, but when Tompkins sailed her back by himself a few weeks later, the autopilots did him in. The first unit failed and the backup was left behind to save weight for buoy racing in Hawaii. Tough luck for Tompkins, who was already too far out to sea to go back. He defaulted to the only solution left: hand steering MUSTANG SALLY back to California, which was an upwind slog of 22 long and arduous days.

Living with limitations

Cruisers who live aboard year-round have slightly different requirements, since the boat also is their home. But they too benefit from less weight so cleaning house in regular intervals is a must. "Keep an eye on the waterline and go through all the stuff at least once a year," Hausner noted. His rule is that anything that hasn't been used since the last cleaning will be given away, bartered or disposed of. "Live simple, buy less," suggested Renoldner, who scrutinizes the on-board energy consumption. "Our biggest energy hogs are autopilot and refrigeration when underway and refrigeration and computer while at anchor. We have three 55W solar panels on the foredeck, which is practical but not necessarily ideal, because of shading issues. They need a new home, either on the dodger or on a separate arch on the stern." In addition they use an Air Breeze wind generator, "a vast improvement over its predecessor," and in emergencies a Honda 1KW generator, which backfills their energy needs when they work on the computer for days on end (as authors and photographers) while anchored out. Goodlander's big secret, which of course isn't so secret: He's a minimalist, but that's perhaps one reason why he is still out there on WILDCARD, a 38-foot S&S sloop he had bought for a song and restored himself. "I have no generator, because I don't have refrigeration," he said. But that's not the only place for sustainable savings. "I haul out once every two years. I went seven years without an engine. Now that I have one I use it sparingly. From Panama to New Zealand I burned 50 gallons of fuel, but I never cranked the engine for electrical needs." He said he gets all his power from renewable energy.

How a limited energy supplies can change habits, became clear to Aebi during her Pacific crossing with her two teenage sons, for whom that was the first bluewater sailing experience. "Typically, the boys required daily outfit changes, but since I'd told them that after Panama there'd be no more machines, that all future laundry would be done by their hands during the crossing, the boys had been waging a competition to see who'd use the least clothes . . . The other shift was with electricity consumption. Between casting off the mooring buoy in Panama and setting the anchor in Hiva Oa, we ran the engine for a total of 14 hours, meaning the batteries were kept charged by solar and wind power, and the boys learned how to conserve. They now automatically turn off lights and fans behind them, and only open the refrigerator a couple of times a day. They now discuss and plan for what needs to go in and out of it! And computer usage is mainly limited to schoolwork and Sailmail, which only really happens when the engine is running because SSB transmissions use tons of juice. Sam now keeps a constant vigil and a running commentary on the amps being consumed and battery voltage remaining, as displayed by the monitor at the chart table. He scolds me and Nicholas if we forget to turn off a light, or leave a computer unattended—this is a huge change for a boy who used to compulsively open the refrigerator door 72 times a day, so often that he'd gained a neighborhood reputation for the affliction."

Keepers and castaways

One moniker that doesn't fit Hausner is "electronics freak." For a long time he didn't even use a VHF radio on his voyages, but he too adapted and added a few choice items to his equipment. "My most important electronic item is the autopilot, because it gives me time to navigate, cook and rest." Next on his list is radar, which he calls highly useful for singlehanders. He sets it so it scans the horizon in 10-minute intervals and returns to energy conserving sleep mode. He also uses different alarm radii, depending on the density of traffic and his alertness. "Most importantly, you should never be so tired that you'd sleep through an acoustic radar alert." Hausner uses GPS, but shuns chartplotters. "Electronic charts might be accurate in highly trafficked areas, but in the third world where commercial shipping is sparse, it's a whole different story. Small islands often are missing and sometimes the charts show reefs where there aren't any." Hausner said he opposes SSB, EPIRB, PLBs, and sat phone. "I don't need it for safety and I'm not desperate for constant communication. But I have a fishfinder, which is helpful for feeling your way into an unknown anchorage at night."

Apropos anchorages: Renoldner said dropping the hook on a coral reef was against the principle of the Sea Nomads. If coral heads are dotting an anchorage, they tie fenders to the anchor chain to lift it up. Hausner, who also used to make a living as a shell diver, thinks that mooring buoys are often deployed to pad the pockets of local authorities, but advocates the protection of sensible areas, especially in popular scuba diving venues. He anchors mostly on sand or at greater depths away from corals.

None of the interviewed cruisers have air conditioning, but all of them were keen on proper ventilation of the cabins. The deck should be painted white to minimize heat absorption in the tropics, and port lights should be installed, so they can be opened when it rains. "It's a design flaw that is quite frequent," Hausner said. In some respects, cruisers are fighting the same battles as landlubbers, especially regarding the reduction of waste. "In 'civilized countries' waste reduction is difficult to achieve, because everything is packaged," Renoldner observed. To her surprise, recycling proved to be difficult in Australia, New Zealand and South Africa. In remote island nations and in the tropics, fresh and unpackaged food is still easier to come by, so the amount of garbage decreases proportionally. Food scraps and other bio-degradable waste goes by the board (with consideration of wind and current in anchorages), while plastic and used oil is collected on board until it can be disposed of in the next port or it is burned on a remote beach. That's common practice among cruisers and quite often a social event.

What about stocking the larder? Live fish, they said, can still be

Photo 14.1 Riding at anchor in a tropical paradise, Wolfgang Hausner's 60-foot catamaran TABOO III floats on her lines. He designed and built the boat that incorporates his ideas of an ideal cruising vessel. *Wolfgang Hausner*

caught with a trolling line, but in many places the number of catches has decreased noticeably over the years. Whatever is caught and can't be eaten fresh, is cut up, cooked and preserved in old glass jars. If done properly, the meat can last up to one year and can be used for sauces, salads and spreads. Flour, rice, and noodles are common staples, but they have to be stowed in Ziploc bags or moisture-proof containers. Fresh veggies that last the longest are onions, cabbage, potatoes, and squash. "It is important to check the food-stuffs often and thoroughly," Renoldner suggested. "If you buy too much, you might end up in an all-you-can-eat contest before something goes bad."

Cruisers also have a well-defined opinion about antifouling paint. Except for Slanec and Renoldner, who have an aluminum boat that has to be treated with copper-free antifouling, effectiveness was the most important consideration. "Antifouling is our drama," Renolder said. "New and environmentally friendly paints force us to scrub the hull every few weeks." Like Hausner, she criticized permissive policies that in some parts of the world have allowed commercial shippers to continue the use of paints that were outlawed for pleasure boats. It is important to understand that "hauling out" for some cruisers (especially those with catamarans or centerboard boats) means sailing up on a sandy beach and work on the hull at low tide.

Even if they renew their bottom paint in a marina in a developing country, chances are it won't have the same facilities and equipment as marinas in the U.S. or Europe do, where environmental regulations are much more restrictive.

One consideration that was brought up repeatedly was equipment quality: "Simple boats have simple problems," Slanec and Renoldner stated. "Buy the best gear you can afford, but stick to KISS. That means fewer repairs and more leisure." Slanec was critical of the quality of the products that often don't stand up to the rigors of everyday use. He proposed that designers and manufacturers of boating accessories "should have to spend one year sailing nonstop, using their creations." Bad hatch seals, low-quality stainless-steel parts, frozen winches, poorly sealed aluminum surfaces, regular failures in electronics, and flashlights that never seem to work when they're most needed top the list of his pet peeves.

What are the redeeming lessons from life on the seven seas without a bottomless kitty?

To paraphrase the Sea Nomads: Sail more, motor less. Repair if you can instead of tossing it into the trash. Buy less, live simply and lead by example. It's what sustainable sailing is all about.

SOURCES:
Tania Aebi: www.taniaaebi.com, www.boatus.com/cruising/
    shangrila
Fatty Goodlander: www.fattygoodlander.com
Seenomaden: www.seenomaden.at
Wolfgang Hausner: www.wolfgang-hausner.com

Index